THE AGES OF STEAM AND ELECTRICITY

Edited by Tim Cooke

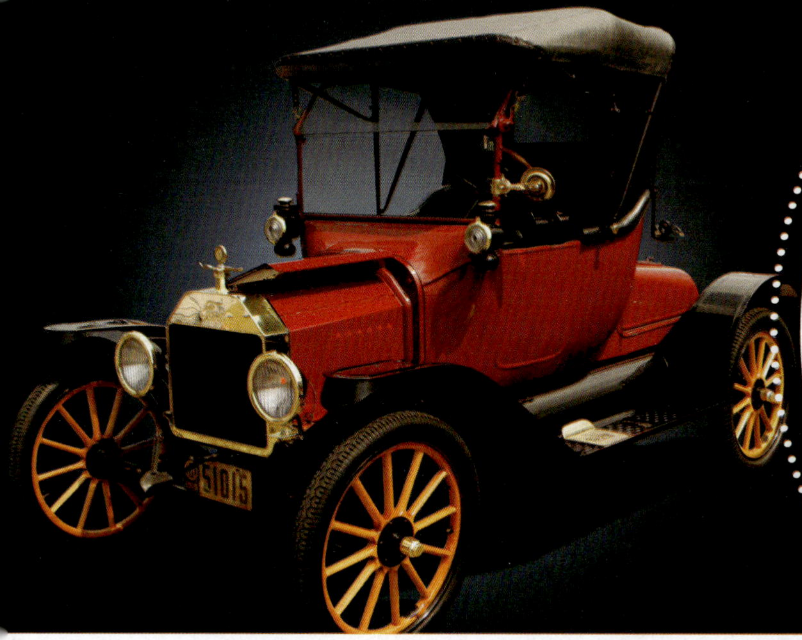

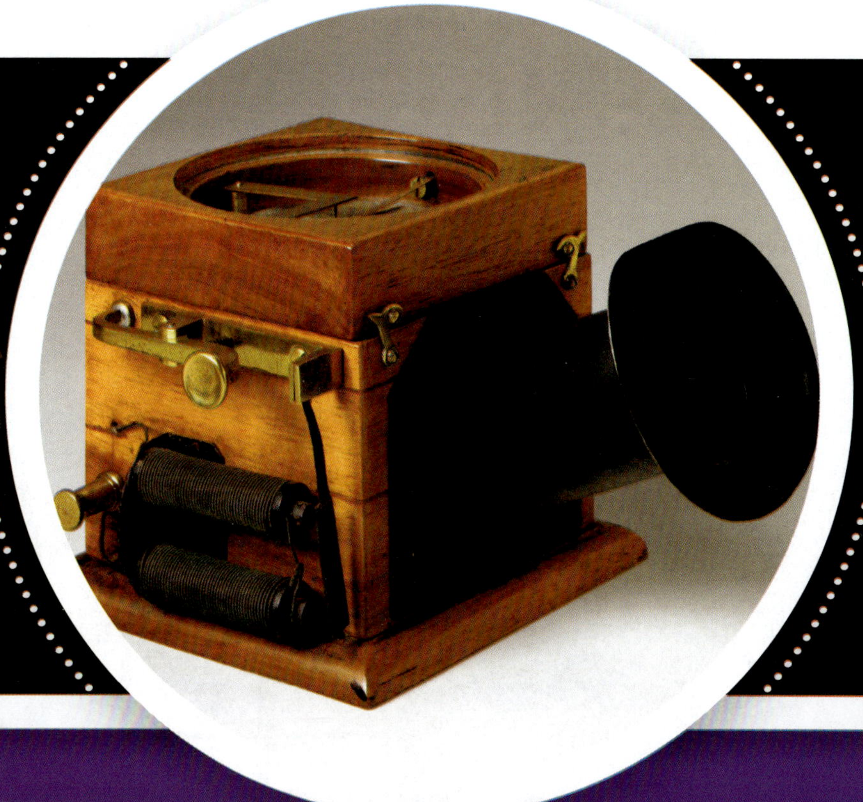

TEACHER RESOURCES

SCIENTIFIC DISCOVERY

LIGHTBOX
openlightbox.com

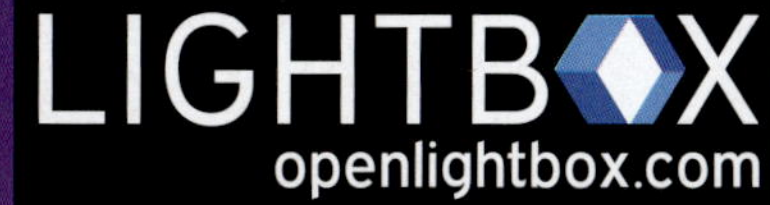

Go to
www.openlightbox.com
and enter this book's unique code.

ACCESS CODE

LBXL2456

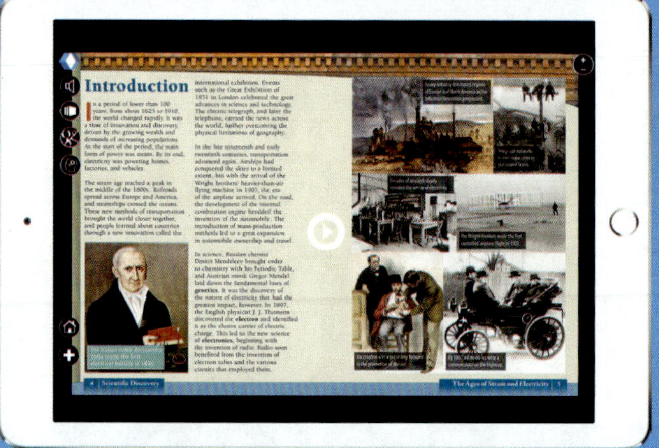

Lightbox is an all-inclusive digital solution for the teaching and learning of curriculum topics in an original, groundbreaking way. Lightbox is based on National Curriculum Standards.

STANDARD FEATURES OF LIGHTBOX

AUDIO High-quality narration using text-to-speech system

VIDEOS Embedded high-definition video clips

ACTIVITIES Printable PDFs that can be emailed and graded

WEBLINKS Curated links to external, child-safe resources

SLIDESHOWS Pictorial overviews of key concepts

TRANSPARENCIES Step-by-step layering of maps, diagrams, charts, and timelines

INTERACTIVE MAPS Interactive maps and aerial satellite imagery

QUIZZES Ten multiple choice questions that are automatically graded and emailed for teacher assessment

KEY WORDS Matching key concepts to their definitions

MORE Extra information and details on the subject

FIRST HAND Letters, diaries, and other primary sources

DOCS Speeches, newspaper articles, and other historical documents

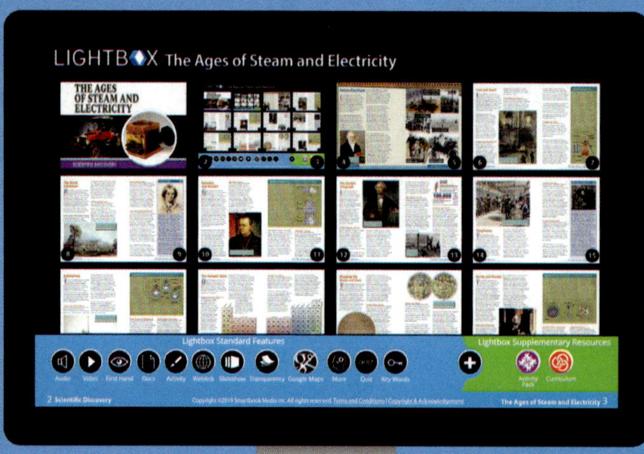

Contents

RUBRIC

Create a Scientific Poster

Students will create a scientific poster on the topic of "The Age of Invention," 1825–1910. An exemplary poster will meet the following criteria:

- The poster has a title that suggests the chosen topic or theme
- The poster presents relevant and accurate information about the topic or theme
- The format of the poster is appropriate to the content, purpose, and audience that it was designed for
- Visuals such as pictures, photographs, charts, tables, scientific drawings, diagrams add to the effectiveness of the poster
- The poster is well organized, and the poster elements work well together
- The use of appropriate graphic design tools, space, color, texture, and shape effectively creates an aesthetically pleasing product
- The poster draws attention
- Language chosen for the poster is accurate, informative, and concise

Introduction

In a period of fewer than 100 years, from about 1825 to 1910, the world changed rapidly. It was a time of innovation and discovery, driven by the growing wealth and demands of increasing populations. At the start of the period, the main form of power was steam. By its end, electricity was powering homes, factories, and vehicles.

The steam age reached a peak in the middle of the 1800s. Railroads spread across Europe and America, and steamships crossed the oceans. These new methods of transportation brought the world closer together, and people learned about countries through a new innovation called the international exhibition. Events such as the Great Exhibition of 1851 in London celebrated the great advances in science and technology. The electric telegraph, and later the telephone, carried the news across the world, further overcoming the physical limitations of geography.

The Italian noble Alessandro Volta made the first electrical battery in 1800.

In the late nineteenth and early twentieth centuries, transportation advanced again. Airships had conquered the skies to a limited extent, but with the arrival of the Wright brothers' heavier-than-air flying machine in 1903, the era of the airplane arrived. On the road, the development of the internal combustion engine heralded the invention of the automobile. The introduction of mass-production methods led to a great expansion in automobile ownership and travel.

In science, Russian chemist Dmitri Mendeleev brought order to chemistry with his Periodic Table, and Austrian monk Gregor Mendel laid down the fundamental laws of **genetics**. It was the discovery of the nature of electricity that had the greatest impact, however. In 1897, the English physicist J.J. Thomson discovered the **electron** and identified it as the elusive carrier of electric charge. This led to the new science of **electronics**, beginning with the invention of radio. Radio soon benefited from the invention of electron tubes and the various circuits that employed them.

Heavy industry dominated regions of Europe and North America as the Industrial Revolution progressed.

Telegraph networks linked major cities in the United States.

Decades of research slowly revealed the nature of electricity.

The Wright Brothers made the first controlled airplane flight in 1903.

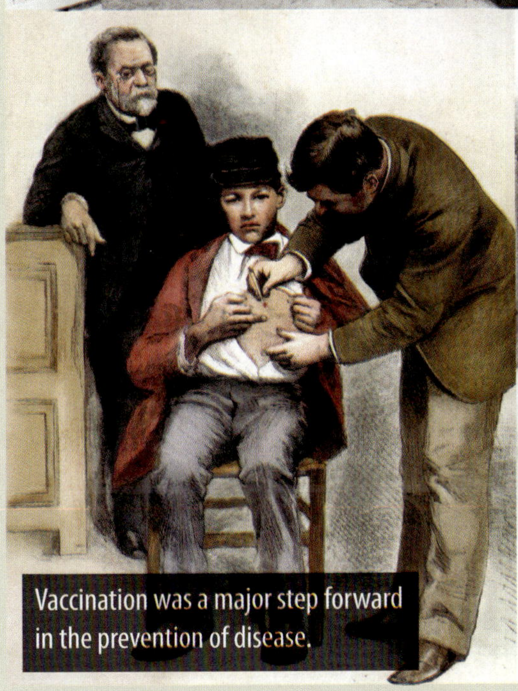

Vaccination was a major step forward in the prevention of disease.

By 1900, automobiles were a common sight on the highway.

ACTIVITIES

Video

The Wright Brothers and Flight
Watch this video on the Wright Brothers and the early days of flight.

1. How dangerous were these early flights? What was the technology for landing these planes?
2. What was the purpose of cranking the propellers of the aircraft to get the engine started? What changes in design can you identify over the first few years of the Wright Brothers' machines?

Weblink

Key Scientific Discoveries in the Ages of Steam and Electricity
Examine this weblink that summarizes the technological and economic changes brought by the Industrial Revolution.

1. Explain the importance of James Watt's condenser for the rapid development of steam power. Describe the importance of investment, patents and legal structures for the creation of the steam locomotive.
2. Describe the relationship between coal and iron in the Industrial Revolution in Great Britain. Why were so many noted early entrepreneurs from religious groups that endured legal disadvantages?

RUBRIC

Writing a Comparative Essay

Students will research online and in the library, and then write a comparative essay to compare coal with two other sources of energy used throughout the world. An exemplary comparative essay will meet the following criteria:

- Consists of a one-paragraph introduction, two or more body paragraphs, and a one-paragraph conclusion
- Introduction includes an engaging lead statement about the topic of the essay, more detailed information about the chosen topic, and a one-sentence thesis that specifically states the essay's argument
- Each body paragraph includes a topic sentence that refers to and supports the thesis, textual evidence of the argument, and an analysis of this evidence
- Body paragraphs end with a transition to the next paragraph
- Conclusion refers to the topic of the essay and the points presented in the body paragraphs, and restates the thesis
- Provides a thorough analysis of the topics in question
- Presents a clear, specific thesis that indicates a high level of critical engagement
- Organizes ideas in a logical manner
- Communicates arguments in a clear, effective manner
- Uses correct spelling, punctuation, and grammar
- Properly integrates any quotations used
- Correctly cites all sources used
- Correctly formats bibliography

Iron and Steel

In about 600 BC, the Chinese developed a type of furnace that was filled with fuel and crushed iron ore while air was forced in at the bottom. This "blast furnace" was hot enough to produce iron in liquid form that could be poured into molds to make large objects by casting. Around 1400 AD, the blast furnace appeared independently in Europe.

By the beginning of the eighteenth century, charcoal was becoming scarce. In 1709, British ironworker Abraham Darby fueled a blast furnace using coke, made by heating coal in a closed oven. Cast iron grew in importance, and in 1779, Darby's family built the first iron bridge in England. Great Britain led the way in ironmaking until about 1870, when Germany and the United States took the lead.

Improving the Process

Cast iron is too brittle for many industrial purposes, so **wrought iron** remained in demand. However, it could only be produced in small amounts. In 1784, a new method was patented by British ironworker Henry Cort. Hot air from a coal fire was directed onto pig iron from a blast furnace, converting the pig iron into wrought iron. The process made wrought iron much cheaper. Demand soared as the iron was used for railroad tracks, bridges, and new iron ships.

The Advent of Steel

In 1856, the British inventor Henry Bessemer devised a process for making steel in large quantities. He used a device called a converter. Steel is iron mixed with small amounts of carbon, which makes it strong and tough.

The Bessemer process made it easier and cheaper to produce steel in furnaces.

A second way to make steel, the Siemens-Martin furnace, came into use from the 1860s. It was an open-hearth furnace with brick chambers at the ends that allowed hot air to pass back and forth. Both these methods were used into the twentieth century.

Steel gradually replaced wrought iron and cast iron for making railroad tracks, large bridges, and steel-framed skyscrapers. Steelmaking became big business in the United States. The decline of wrought iron was not immediate, however. As late as 1889, the Eiffel Tower in Paris was built from wrought iron.

Improving Steel

In 1889, it was shown that an **alloy** of steel with nickel made a very tough metal. It was adopted for armor-plating warships. In 1912, British metallurgist Harold Brearley discovered stainless steels, which include chromium and certain types of nickel.

Other existing metals and alloys also continued to play an important role. Brass was used increasingly from the eighteenth century onward for steam-engine cylinders, boilers, and domestic plumbing. The need for pure copper increased dramatically from about 1880 because of its use in electric wiring. Tin was in demand from the 1850s, when canning food using tin-plated iron became a major industry. Lead became important in the twentieth century, when it was used in automobile batteries.

The Blast Furnace

Modern blast furnaces are steel cylinders lined with heat-resistant bricks. Giant stoves heat the air that is blasted in at the bottom of the furnace through pipes called tuyères. Wagons take ore, coke, and limestone to the top of the furnace. A small "bell" is lowered to let the material into the first compartment. The small bell closes the top before a large bell drops to let the material into the furnace. The coke burns first, reacting with oxygen in the air to form carbon monoxide gas. This gas removes oxygen from the iron ore, turning it into metallic iron which, in turn, becomes molten in the intense heat. The molten iron is removed through a hole at the bottom of the furnace.

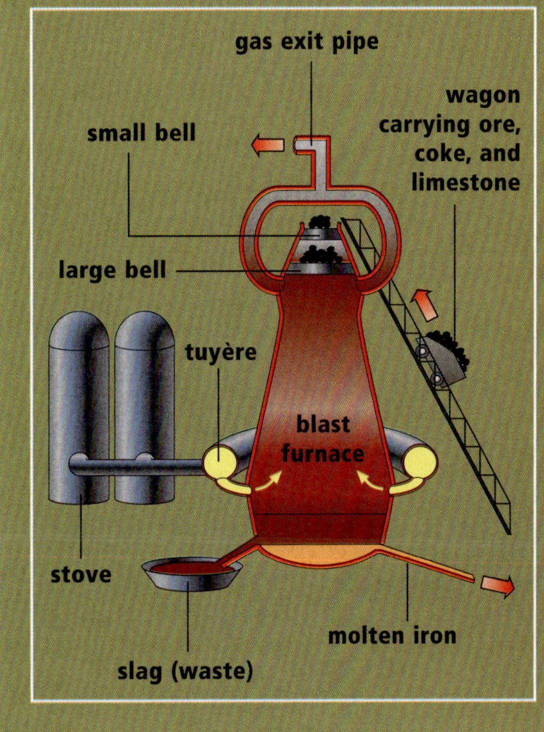

ACTIVITIES

Transparency

The Blast Furnace

Examine the diagram showing the key parts of a blast furnace.

1. Why is limestone used as part of the material put into the top of the furnace? Describe the advantages of coke over coal in the process.
2. Explain how the waste is separated from the molten iron. Why is the gas produced as a by-product carbon monoxide and not carbon dioxide?

Weblink

The Development of Cast Iron and Steel

Review the weblink that describes the relationship between coal and iron in the industrial revolution.

1. Describe reasons why the British government would have banned the use of wood for making charcoal. How was coke first invented?
2. Why was the sulphur in some types of coal a problem in blast furnaces? Summarize the key stages of the Bessemer process.

The Great Exhibition

Prince Albert, husband of Queen Victoria, became president of Britain's Royal Society of Arts in 1843. Six years later, he came up with the idea of an exhibition to show off the "Industries of All Nations." At the time, manufacturing industry was concentrated in Britain, which was justifiably described as the workshop of the world. Queen Victoria put up money for the project. Leading manufacturers also contributed funds to make up the £80,000 needed.

English architect Joseph Paxton received the commission to design the building to house the exhibition. It was constructed in Hyde Park, London. To demonstrate the technology of the era, Paxton designed a structure built from prefabricated iron sections and glass. The structure soon came to be known as the Crystal Palace. Paxton, the son of a farmer, had begun his working life as a gardener before becoming a designer of hothouses and conservatories. This early work helped inspire the Crystal Palace.

Influential Design

The Crystal Palace was "great" by any standards. It was 1,847 feet (563 meters) long, 407 feet (124 m) wide, and more than 100 feet (30.5 m) high. More than 3,000 iron columns and 2,000 girders supported 903,840 square feet (84,000 sq m) of glass. That is nearly enough glass to cover 17 football fields. The Crystal Palace influenced the design of many mainline railroad stations in Europe.

The Great Exhibition is historically seen as a highpoint of British colonial power.

Large and Small

There were about 14,000 exhibitors, showing more than 100,000 examples of manufactured goods, including everything from printing presses, railroad locomotives, and hydraulic machinery to items as small as cutlery and jewelry. The 560 U.S. exhibits included Cyrus McCormick's reaper, a machine for harvesting wheat, and Samuel Colt's revolver, a handgun. The French provided 1,700 exhibits. The exhibition remained open for six months, and received more than 6 million visitors. It made a profit.

International Exhibitions

The Great Exhibition was the first of several similar exhibitions or world fairs held in cities such as Vienna, Paris, New York, and Chicago. One of the grandest was held in Chicago in 1893. The World's Columbian Exhibition celebrated the 400th anniversary of the arrival in America of Christopher Columbus. It was held in 150 buildings that became known as the White City, built around a lagoon that opened off Lake Michigan. The unified classical style of the exhibition's buildings began what was known as the Beaux-Arts period of architecture, which dominated major U.S. city centers for the next 40 years.

The original Crystal Palace was taken down in 1852 and rebuilt on a hill in south London. It was used for exhibitions and other shows until it was destroyed by fire in 1936. The London district where it once stood is still known as Crystal Palace.

A Writer Visits

The English writer Charlotte Brontë visited the Great Exhibition twice, and after her second visit wrote a friend about her experiences. Brontë was one of three sisters from the village of Haworth in Yorkshire in northern England who became famous novelists. They originally published their books under men's names in order to avoid prejudice against female writers. Charlotte had a great success with her novel *Jane Eyre*, which was published in 1847. After this success, her publisher encouraged her to visit London regularly to meet with other leading writers of the day. It was on one of those trips that she described visiting the Crystal Palace. Charlotte's sister Emily was the author of the romantic novel *Wuthering Heights*. The third sister, Anne Brontë, was mainly known for her book *The Tenant of Wildfell Hall*.

ACTIVITIES

First Hand

Charlotte Bronte describes her visit to The Crystal Palace

Examine the first-hand account by this novelist.

1. Why would the crowd be subdued and not making much noise? Describe what the author finds so impressive about the exhibition.
2. Explain why the author has no negative thoughts about the "vast, strange and new" things that she was seeing. Describe how other authors were critical of the results of industrialization.

Weblink

The Great Exhibition

Review the website on the origins of the Great Exhibition of 1851.

1. Why was there such enthusiasm for such exhibitions? What percentage of the 100,000 exhibits at the Great Exhibition could have been made 100 years previously?
2. Describe any equivalents to the Great Exhibition in North America during the 1800s. Why did a new type of workman called the "navvie" (navigator) emerge during the industrial revolution?

RUBRIC

Creating a Timeline

Students will explore the topic of genetics from Darwin's voyage on the Beagle to the present day, and create a timeline to present their research on scientific events connected to this topic. An exemplary timeline will meet the following criteria:

- Includes the most significant events pertaining to the topic to be compared and analyzed
- Includes interesting events
- Uses accurate information for all events, including date, location, and major details
- Orders the events in a chronological sequence
- Describes each event with accurate, vivid, and specific details
- Presents the topic from three or more perspectives
- Inspires the reader to ask thoughtful questions regarding the events and perspectives presented in the timeline
- Uses correct spelling, grammar, and punctuation
- Presents the timeline in a visually attractive and striking manner
- Presents the timeline in a neat, organized manner that is logical and easy to follow
- Uses creativity to present the timeline in an engaging manner
- Effectively communicates historical information relating to the topic
- Supports each event with reliable sources
- Includes a correctly formatted bibliography of all sources used to create the timeline

Genetics and Mendel

Gregor Mendel was born at Heinzendorf in Austrian Silesia, now Hyncice in the Czech Republic. He studied in college before becoming an Augustinian monk in 1843. By 1868, he was abbot of the monastery at Brünn, or Brno. Mendel became interested in hybrid plants and began to breed pea plants in 1856. In the next six years, he grew 30,000 plants, which he fertilized by transferring pollen from the flowers of one plant to those of another. He crossed tall plants with short plants, and then counted the number of tall and short plants in the next and later generations. He found that all first-generation plants were tall, but that the second generation contained both tall plants and short plants in the ratio of 3 to 1.

Mendel concluded that every plant receives two "factors" of inheritance, one from each parent. He worked out that, in the first generation of peas, each plant receives one factor for tallness from the tall parent and one factor for shortness from the short parent. All the offspring were tall, so the tallness factor was dominant over the shortness factor. The shortness factor is described as recessive. Recessive factors can, however, become apparent when two occur in a single plant, as happened in short plants of the second generation.

Mendel's Laws

These observations led Mendel to propose two laws. His law of segregation states that the two factors controlling each hereditary characteristic pass into separate germ cells, the eggs and sperm. Mendel's law of independent assortment states that the pairs of factors segregate independently during the formation of germ cells. In 1865, the Natural History Society in Brünn published Mendel's results. Nobody took much notice. As Mendel's monastical duties increased, science began to occupy less time and importance in his life.

The significance of Mendel's research was overlooked because he was far from any scientific centers.

Genetics in Plants

The diagram shows how Mendel's laws predict the colors produced by crossing purple-flowered peas with white-flowered peas. Purple is dominant, and the first generation produced by planting seeds from the cross are all purple. These are the F1 phenotypes. The phenotype is the appearance of a plant or animal that results from its genetic makeup, known as its genotype. All of these peas have purple flowers. When this generation is interbred, the second generation, or F2 phenotypes, has purple or white flowers in the ratio 3 to 1. This can be explained by assuming that the allele for purple (A) is dominant over the allele for white (a). Among the F2 phenotypes, one-quarter are aa and purple in color, two-quarters are Aa and also purple, since A is dominant. Only one-quarter are white (aa). White turns up only when two "a" recessive alleles occur together.

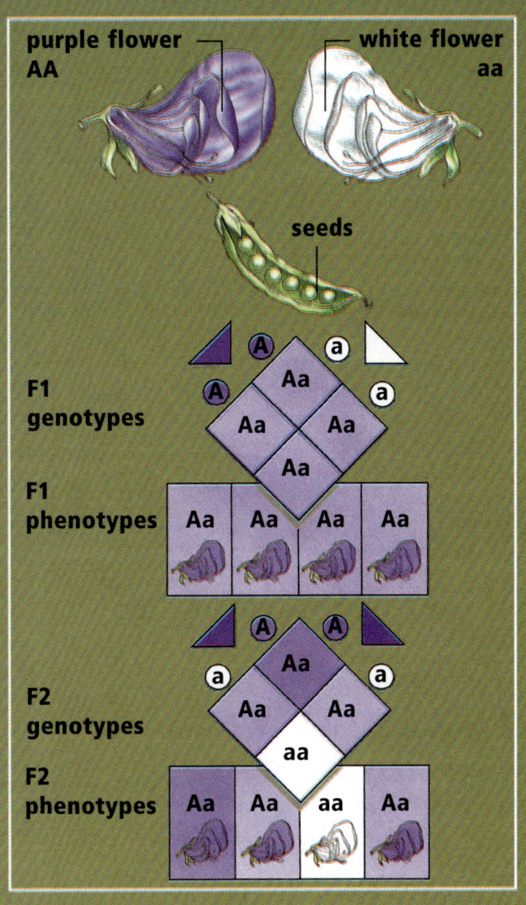

Today, Mendel's "factors" are called alleles, which are alternative forms of a **gene**. Any body cell of an organism has two alleles of each gene, one inherited from each parent, occupying the same place on a chromosome. Usually one allele is dominant, and the other is recessive. A germ cell, or gamete, has only one allele. When fertilization occurs, the two alleles form a new individual that inherits characteristics from each parent. The appearance of the new individual depends on which characteristic, if any, is dominant.

Mendel's Legacy

In the 1890s, after Mendel's death, several botanists independently studied inheritance in plants. In the Netherlands, Dutch botanist Hugo de Vries came up with results identical to Mendel's. His discovery of Mendel's obscure publication prompted him to announce his own results in 1900. The German Karl Correns and Austrian Erich von Tschermak-Seysenegg also published observations that confirmed Mendel had been right. Between them, these four scientists had founded the science of genetics.

ACTIVITIES

Transparency

Genetics in Plants

Examine the diagram on Mendel's law of the way that characteristics are inherited.

1. Why were pea plants so useful as the object of Mendel's study? Describe how Mendel's work relates to the theories of Charles Darwin.
2. Why were Mendel's ideas disregarded during his lifetime? Compare Mendel with another scientist whose ideas were overlooked while he or she was alive.

Weblink

Mendel's Principles of Inheritance

Review this weblink concerning Gregor Mendel's experiments.

1. Summarize the traits in pea plants that Mendel investigated. Why did he begin with pure-breeding pea plants?
2. Why are the recessive traits the ones that can cause surprises for breeders in subsequent generations? Explain what an allele is.

The Electric Telegraph

In 1804, shortly after the invention of the electric battery, the Catalan scientist Don Francisco Salvá i Campillo tried using electricity to send signals. He devised a system using wires connected to electrodes immersed in acidified water, which bubbled to identify specific letters. In 1809, German physicist Samuel von Sömmering made a similar electrolytic telegraph with 35 wires, which operated over a distance of 1.9 miles (3 km). In England, in 1816, inventor Francis Ronalds modified the system so that it needed only two wires to operate.

Samuel Morse was a famous portrait painter before he became an inventor.

Improving the System

In 1820, Danish physicist Hans Ørsted found that an electric current flowing along a wire deflected a pivoted magnetic needle placed nearby. By 1835, Joseph Henry had made a telegraph using pulses of electricity to represent coded letters. The pulses caused a piece of iron to "click" as it responded to an electromagnet at the receiver. U.S. inventor Samuel Morse later based his own system on Henry's idea.

Meanwhile, in 1832, Russian inventor Pavel Schilling used Ørsted's discovery to make the first magnetized needle telegraph. It used six wires, and the electric current magnetized coils that deflected needles above them. German physicists Karl Gauss and Wilhelm Weber saw Schilling's demonstration. In 1833, they sent signals over 1.9 miles (3 km), using a two-wire, single-needle telegraph. In England, four years later, William Cooke and Charles Wheatstone patented a needle telegraph with six wires. It used five needles that indicated letters on a diamond-shaped board. This telegraph was installed on part of the British Great Western Railway in 1838.

In 1843, the number of wires was reduced to three, and by 1845, they had simplified the receiver so that only one needle was required. By 1852, nearly 4,040 miles (6,500 km) of Britain's railroads were equipped with telegraphic communications.

Messages in Code

Samuel Morse demonstrated his single-wire telegraph in 1838. Its first commercial application was in 1844, over the railroad line along the 37-mile (60-km) route between the cities of Washington and Baltimore. Morse's telegraph was an improvement of Henry's ideas, but Morse's great contribution to communication was his invention of a code of dots and dashes to stand for letters and digits. **Morse code** became the universally accepted way of sending telegraph messages. Later, it also became the standard method for sending radio messages. The final version of the Morse code was mainly the work of Morse's assistant, Alfred Vail.

By the early 1900s, much of the world was connected by telegraph.

$100

COST PER MILE (1.6 KM)

Erecting telegraph wires cost at least $100 per mile (1.6 km). In remote or difficult terrain, the cost could be as high as $200 per mile (1.6 km).

100,000

MILES (160,000 KM)

The length of telegraph wires in the United States by 1866.

Linking the World

By the mid-1800s, telegraph lines criss-crossed North America as well as Europe. Cables were also laid beneath areas of water, including New York Harbor in 1845, and the English Channel in 1851. In 1855, English-born U.S. inventor David Hughes produced a printing telegraph, in which the sender tapped the message on a keyboard, and a similar machine at the receiver automatically typed the message as it arrived, letter by letter. In the United States in 1856, the New York and Mississippi Valley Printing Telegraph Company changed its name to Western Union Telegraph Company to signify the joining of telegraph lines from west to east. From then onward, the telegraph was the main method of local and international communication until it was superseded by telephone and radio.

ACTIVITIES

Document

First Message Sent and Signed by Samuel Morse and Paper Tape Return Message

Examine the first telegraph message sent by Morse code.

1. Why did it take five years for Congress to fund Morse's invention after the first public demonstration? Can you describe a modern system of communication that is similar to Morse's dots and dashes in its use of just two elements to encode information?
2. Describe the infrastructure needed to support Morse's telegraph. How rapidly could telegraph operators send messages?

Weblink

The History of the Electric Telegraph

Review this website on the history of the electric telegraph.

1. Why did inventors in the early 1800s apply their research into electricity to devising a form of communication? Describe the contemporary industries or activities that might have benefited from the telegraph.
2. Explain the importance of the electromagnet in the development of the telegraph. Describe how the electric telegraph was superior to the optical telegraph, which used flags and semaphore signaling.

Early telephone calls passed through centralized exchanges, where they were then directed to the appropriate home.

Telephones

The first telephone was demonstrated in 1861 by the German inventor Philipp Reis. It carried voice signals over a wire by converting acoustic vibrations to electrical signals. Reis used his invention largely as a teaching aid to illustrate how sound travels in waves. On the same day, February 14, 1876, Scotsman Alexander Graham Bell and the American Elisha Gray both filed patents for devices for sending speech along wires.

By October 1876, Bell, who had emigrated to Canada and then moved to the United States, had demonstrated his device operating over a distance of 2 miles (5 km). Bell offered his patent to the Western Union Telegraph Company, but the company saw no future in the idea and turned it down. Bell was almost the only person to see the commercial possibilities of the telephone. He set up his own company in order to produce and market his invention. By 1887, there were more than 150,000 telephones in the United States, proving Western Union wrong.

Louder Signals

Speech quality with Bell's original telephone was good over short distances. Calls over a longer distance were faint, however, because the microphone inside the telephone did not amplify, or strengthen, the signal. Then, in 1886, the American inventor Thomas Alva Edison produced the carbon microphone. Edison's microphone has small granules of carbon in the mouthpiece that vibrate in time with the speech pattern, converting the sound waves into electrical energy that can be transmitted down a wire. Telephones with carbon microphones installed could now make long-distance calls, though at the expense of slightly poorer sound quality.

Connecting Cities

Another important development in 1886 was the creation of the American Telephone and Telegraph Company (AT&T). The new company was a subsidiary of Bell's own company. From 1887, AT&T opened trunk, or long-distance, telephone lines across the United States. By the start of the twentieth century, most towns in the East were connected to one another by telephone.

The telephone was to become a momentous instrument in the history of communication. Not only could people now hear each other's voices clearly across great distances, but the process was almost instantaneous. The telephone linked the world into a single huge network.

Alexander Graham Bell

The invention of the telephone remains the subject of controversy. Alexander Graham Bell and Elisha Gray both filed their patents on the same day. Three days later, on February 17, 1876, Bell made the first recorded telephone call. He spoke to his assistant in the next room, saying "Mr Watson, come here. I want to see you." Although Bell made the phone call using a water transmitter like that proposed by Gray, he at once abandoned such technology and concentrated on developing the electromagnetic telephone, which he had originally patented. That has not prevented Elisha Gray and many people since from arguing that Bell had stolen the idea for the telephone. In 1876, Bell conducted experiments near his home in Western Ontario, Canada, that involved sending signals over distances of 4 miles (6.4 km) or more. In 1877, Bell set up his own Bell Telephone Company in the United States to build phone lines and sell telephones.

ACTIVITIES

Video

Alexander Graham Bell Counting in 1885

Examine this video of Alexander Graham Bell's voice.

1. Why is there a background hiss to the recording? What are the crackles in the recording caused by? Describe the process.
2. Explain how Bell's electromagnetic telephone was an improvement on Elisha Gray's water transmitter.

Weblink

Thomas Alva Edison's Carbon Microphone

Review this account of Edison's improvements to the telephone.

1. Describe how Edison devised the idea of a carbon-based technology. Why was it important that carbon provided a sensitive, variable resistance? Why would anthracite coal have produced a better result than softer coal?
2. Why did Western Union turn down Bell's invention? Describe the relationship between the invention of the telephone and its commercial development as a method of mass communication.

Submarines

The first recorded attempt to build a submarine dates from 1620. Dutchman Cornelis Drebbel covered a rowing boat with greased leather and maneuvered it below the surface of the Thames River in London. In 1776, American student David Bushnell built a barrel-shaped, one-man submarine called *Turtle*, with two hand-operated propellers. During the American Revolution, Turtle was used in a failed attack on a British ship in New York Harbor.

Successes and Failures

A more successful submarine was built by U.S. engineer Robert Fulton in 1801. The *Nautilus* was built of copper plates on an iron framework and could remain underwater for three hours. In 1855, German soldier Wilhelm Bauer built a larger submarine that made more than 130 dives before it sank. In 1863, Horace Hunley copied Fulton's design to build a submarine for the Confederacy. Eight men worked a crankshaft to turn the propeller. Hunley and his crew died when the vessel sank during a trial. The vessel was raised, and used to attack a Union ship in Charleston Harbor in 1864. It sank again when its explosive ram got stuck in the ship's hull.

In 1863, the French engineer Simon Bourgeois built a test submarine powered by **compressed air**. In 1888, engineer Gustave Zédé completed an electric-powered vessel for the French navy. Other inventors experimented with steam propulsion.

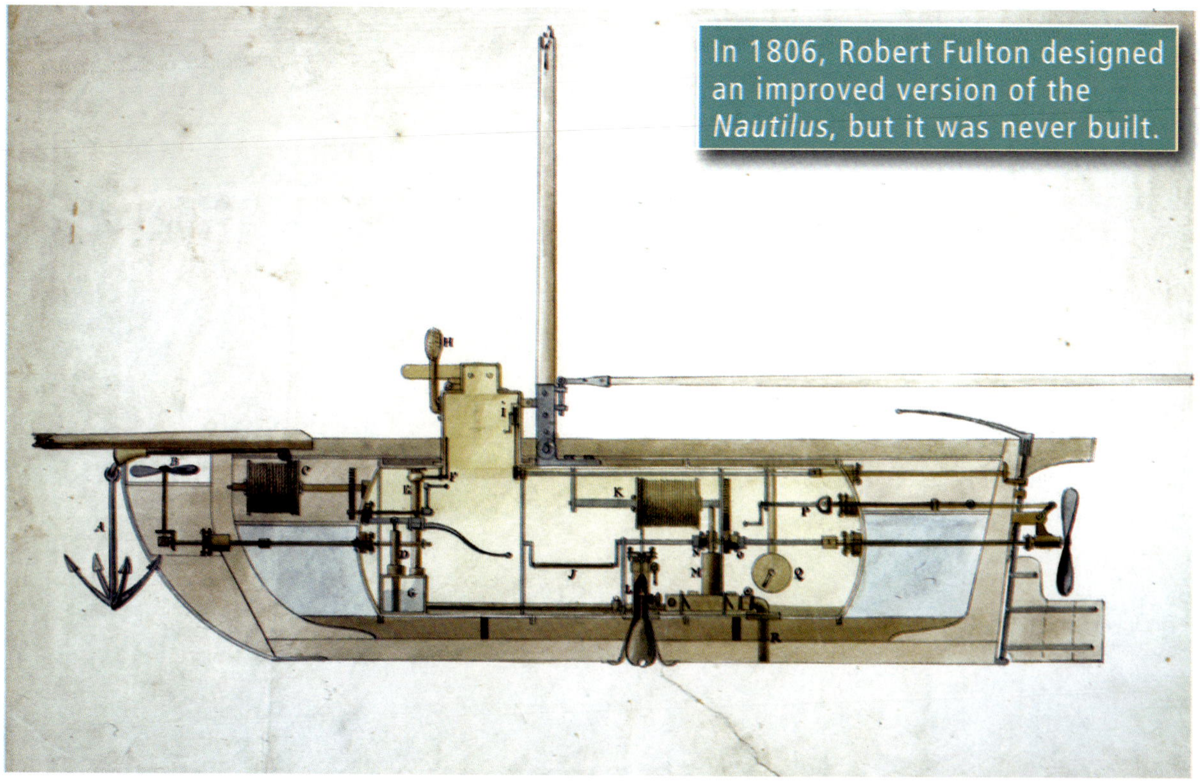

In 1806, Robert Fulton designed an improved version of the *Nautilus*, but it was never built.

Rising and Sinking

A submarine has a twin hull. The space between the two hulls holds water that acts as **ballast** to keep the vessel submerged. When the submarine floats at the surface, the ballast tanks are empty. To make the submarine sink, the lower valves are opened. Seawater enters the ballast tanks, while the upper valves open to let air out. As a result, the submarine becomes heavier than the water it displaces, and it sinks. In order to make the submarine rise again, the upper valves are closed, and compressed air forces water out of the ballast tanks through the lower valves. The submarine can be "trimmed," with the right amount of ballast in the tanks to keep it floating just below the surface of the water.

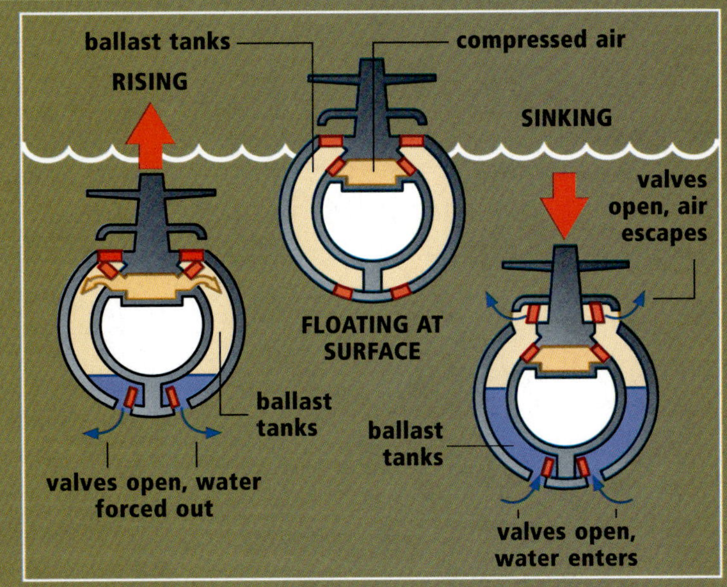

New Forms of Propulsion

Irish-American John Holland solved the propulsion problem. Financed by revolutionaries who wanted Irish independence from the British, Holland built submarines that used gasoline engines for surface propulsion and electric motors when submerged. A series of developments resulted in the *Holland VI* in 1898. It carried a self-propelled torpedo and a deck gun. The U.S. Navy bought the vessel in 1900. Later, "Hollands" were fitted with a periscope, designed in 1902. Holland sold six boats to the U.S. Navy and received orders from the British, Japanese, and Russian navies.

Underwater Weapons

David Bushnell devised the first mine, an underwater explosive device, in 1775. It was not until 1843 that U.S. inventor Samuel Colt successfully detonated a mine underwater, making it a potent weapon. The torpedo was the joint invention of Englishman Robert Whitehead and the Austrian Giovanni Luppis. In 1866, Whitehead built an underwater missile driven by compressed air. The missile detonated when it struck a ship's hull, holing it beneath the waterline and causing the ship to sink. Although widely used in World War I (1914–1918), torpedoes were unreliable weapons.

ACTIVITIES

Transparency

Rising and Sinking

Examine the diagram on buoyancy in submarines.

1. Review the history of submarine construction. When did seawater become the preferred ballast? Is using compressed air to force water out liable to deplete the air within the submarine?
2. In avoiding attack, does the water ballast process need to be supplemented to allow the craft to get deeper more quickly?

Weblink

Early Submarines

Examine the weblink on the history of underwater craft.

1. Why did inventors continue to try to build working submarines, even though the early results were so disastrous? Summarize the ways that early submarine designers tried to find a workable ballast technology.
2. Describe the various methods for sinking enemy vessels that early submarines deployed. Explain the weakness of oars to propel early submarines.

The Periodic Table

Dmitri Mendeleev was born in Tobolsk, Siberia. He went to school in St. Petersburg, and qualified as a teacher in 1855. He later studied chemistry before taking up a university post in St. Petersburg. In 1869, Mendeleev began to write a textbook on chemistry.

Organizing the Elements

Wishing to find some order in the apparent jumble of chemical elements, Mendeleev wrote the name of each on a card. He tried dealing the cards in "hands," like playing cards. He arranged the elements in order of increasing atomic weight, which is the average mass of each atom of an element. If he started a new row of cards every eighth element, those with similar chemical properties fell one above the other in columns. Looking at the horizontal rows, Mendeleev saw that properties tended to recur along each row. He called this "periodicity," and named his new grid of rows and columns the Periodic Table. The arrangement allowed him to include in the table additional "missing" elements that were still to be discovered. He even predicted the chemical and physical properties of these elements, such as their atomic weights and melting points. His predictions were confirmed by the discovery in 1875 of gallium, which fit in a gap beneath aluminum. The discovery of scandium in 1879 and germanium in 1886 filled more gaps. By 1914, there were only seven remaining gaps in the Periodic Table up to element 92.

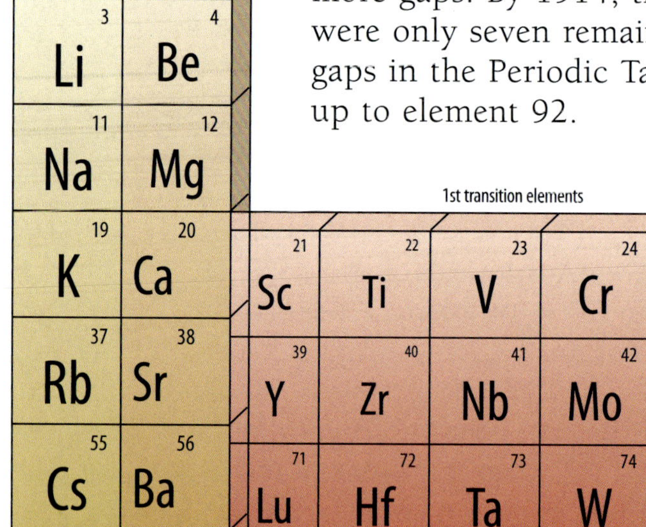

The system of using a letter or letters to denote each element in the Periodic Table had been introduced by Swedish chemist Jöns Berzelius in 1818. Fe is iron, for example, while O stands for oxygen.

ACTIVITIES

Atomic Structure

The modern Periodic Table is better described as being arranged by atomic number rather than atomic weight. The atomic number is the total number of protons in an atom of any element. Chemists now refer to atomic weights as relative atomic masses.

Mendeleev could not explain the periodicity of the elements. That had to await an understanding of the structure of atoms, particularly the way in which electrons arrange themselves around the nucleus of an atom. By the second quarter of the twentieth century, chemists realized that the Periodic Table reflects the atomic structures of the elements as electrons fill up shells around the nucleus.

All chemical reactions involve electrons, particularly an element's outer electrons. The Periodic Table enables chemists to predict what reactions are possible, which are likely to take place in ordinary conditions, and which will require extra effort such as higher temperatures, higher pressures, or catalysts. In 1955, the newly discovered element 101 was named mendelevium in honor of Mendeleev and his work.

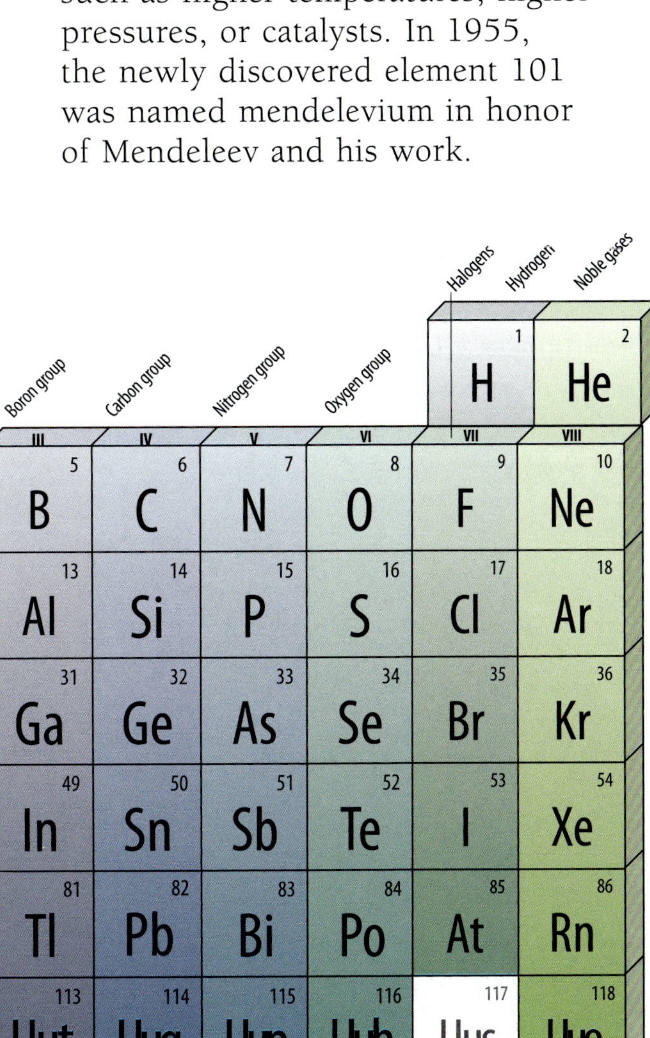

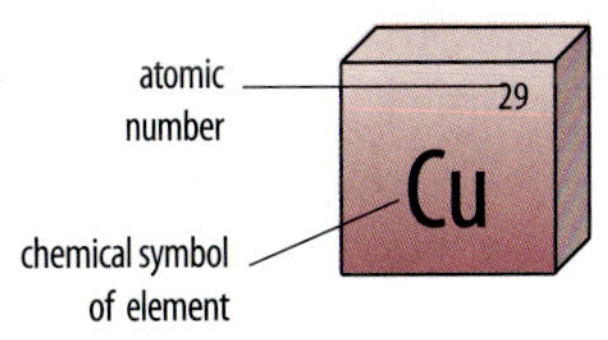

Transparency

The Periodic Table

Analyze the rationale behind the organization of the Periodic Table.

1. Why are the Lanthanoid and Actinoid series included in different lines below the main table? Could there be a better way of viewing the table using a three dimensional model?
2. What is the difference between metals and non-metals? Why are the seven gases on the right-hand column of the table called the Noble Gases?

Weblink

How Dmitri Mendeleev Invented His Periodic Table in a Dream

Read the link about how Mendeleev struggled with the idea of creating the periodic table.

1. Were other people working on the idea of a periodic table during the 1800s? How old is the idea that all matter is created of tiny particles that combine in different ways?
2. Science is supposed to be about hard facts and straight thinking, and yet Mendeleev seemed to need to dream about the table to get it right. How can this be explained scientifically? Are there other examples of scientists who dreamed of a solution to a major problem? Why might dream and rest be an important part of problem solving? Explain and defend your responses.

RUBRIC

Analyzing a Scientific Video

Students will watch and assess a video related to a scientific discovery, and write an analysis of the video. An exemplary video analysis will meet the following criteria.

- Identifies the purpose of the video
- Identifies the intended audience of the video
- Identifies the video as a primary or secondary source
- Discusses the scientific and social context of the video
- Describes how the content of the video is presented
- Summarizes the information and opinions presented in the video
- Analyzes the quality of the content presented in the video
- Assesses the effectiveness of the video
- Determines whether the images and graphics used in the video relate to the content
- Determines whether the video is easy to follow and understand
- Gives the analysis a clear and consistent purpose
- Organizes the analysis in a logical, effective manner
- Presents a strong, clear argument about the video
- Provides strong and accurate details to support the argument about the video
- Considers other perspectives on the purpose and effectiveness of the video
- Cites all sources used in the analysis

Mapping the Moon and Mars

The most powerful telescope used by Galileo Galilei at the start of the 1600s gave him an image of the Moon that was at best six times the size it appears to the naked eye. Even so, the image showed that the mottled surface features of the Moon are caused by mountains and craters. The Flemish cartographer Michael Langrenus published the first detailed map of the Moon in 1645. He introduced the idea of naming lunar mountains and other features for astronomers and famous scientists. Like other people of his time, he thought that the dark areas were expanses of water, and called many of them *mare*, Latin for seas. By 1836, English astronomer Francis Baily confirmed the existence of the large mountains by analyzing the phenomenon now known as Baily's beads. Observing the Moon during an eclipse of the Sun, he noticed a "row of lucid points, like a string of bright beads" around the curved edge of the Moon. Baily correctly interpreted them as being caused by sunlight shining through valleys between tall mountains at the Moon's rim.

Lunar Photographs

In 1839, pioneer French photographer Louis Daguerre included the Moon in a daguerreotype, or early type of photograph. In 1840, English-born U.S. scientist John Draper made daguerreotypes of the Moon. Faster-acting film made Moon photography easier, but hand-drawn maps based on observation were produced until the late nineteenth century. Close-up Moon photography only came in the twentieth century. Detailed pictures were taken in the 1950s and 1960s by Soviet probes and NASA's Ranger missions.

In the 1800s, maps of the Moon were made by carefully observing the lunar surface through telescopes.

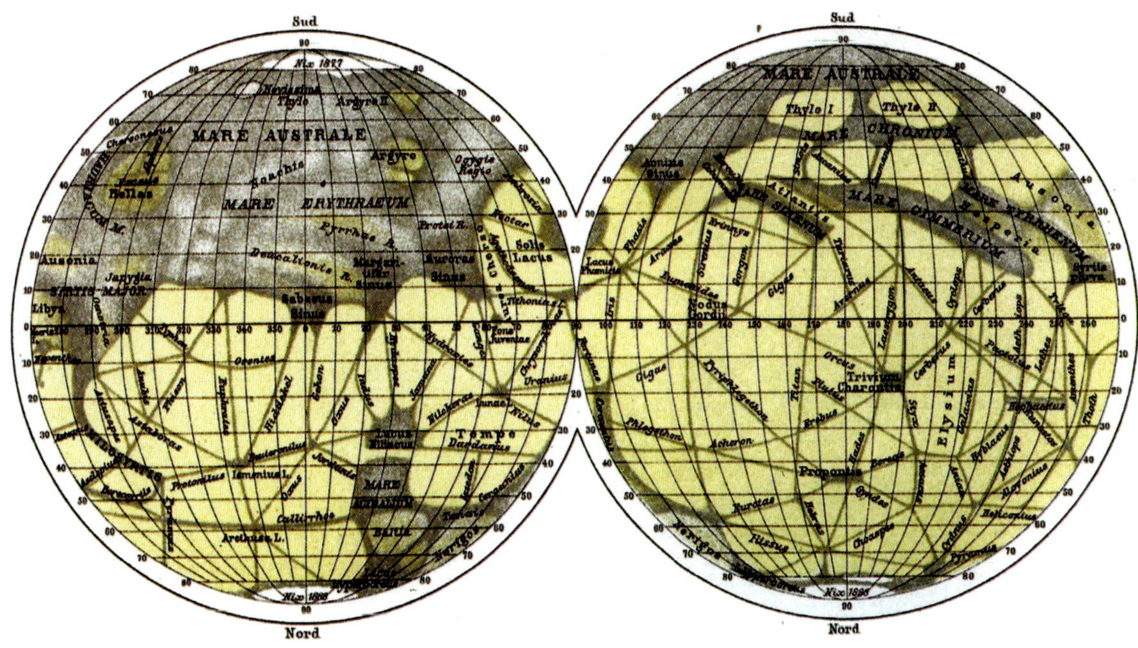

ACTIVITIES

Document

Langrenus' Map of the Moon, 1645

Review this first detailed map of the Moon.

1. Why were seventeenth century astronomers accurate in describing the Moon's mountains, but wrong in describing the areas they called "seas?" Was Langrenus' telescope an improvement on that of Galileo?
2. Explain how seventeenth century astronomers fitted the Moon into their structure of the solar system. Did they believe it circled Earth?

Video

Planetary Cartography

Examine the video about the mapping of the Moon and the planets.

1. Why was the first map of Mars not made until the 1800s? Explain what strength of telescope would be needed to view the surface of Mars.
2. Why are the phases of the Moon a problem for lunar cartographers? How do lunar cartographers deal with this? Describe examples.

Observing Mars

Mars has always held a fascination for people on Earth, particularly the possibility that there might be life on the "Red Planet." In 1666, Italian astronomer Giovanni Cassini pointed out the existence of "ice caps" at the north and south poles of Mars. Dark areas on the planet's surface were first thought to be seas, and then dried-up seabeds.

Then, in 1877, Italian astronomer Giovanni Schiaparelli drew a map of Mars on which he marked what he called "channels." The Italian word *canali* was translated into English as "canals." Their existence led U.S. amateur astronomer Percival Lowell to identify the "canals" as an irrigation system built by Martians to carry water from the ice caps to the dry equatorial regions. Lowell took the first photographs of Mars in 1905, using the telescope at his observatory in Arizona. Modern astronomers regard the Martian canals as a historical curiosity. This opinion was confirmed by the U.S. Mariner 4 probe of 1965 and the Mars series of 1971. The "ice" in the ice caps is now thought to consist mainly of frozen carbon dioxide.

The features of Mars were named using the same conventions as the features on the Moon.

35

JESUIT PRIESTS

Features on the Moon are named for scientists, including 35 Jesuit priests who were also astronomers.

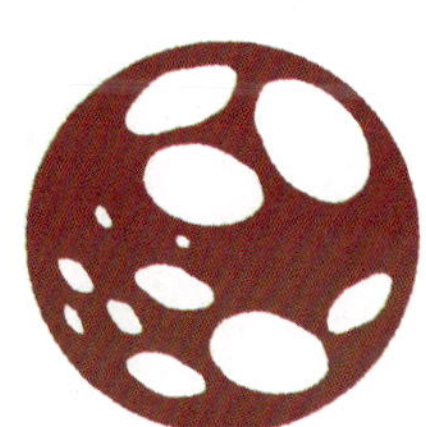

5,185

GIANT CRATERS

The Moon has millions of small craters, but only about 5,185 are more than 12.5 miles (20 km) across.

RUBRIC

Analyzing a Scientific Biography

Students will research the life of Louis Pasteur and present their findings. An exemplary biographical analysis will meet the following criteria:

- Illustrates strong knowledge of the subject
- Identifies the author of the biography
- Describes why the subject of the biography is important
- Contains information about the time and place in which the subject was born
- Lists important events in the subject's life
- Explains how events in the subject's life impacted him or her
- Makes inferences about the subject based on events in his or her life
- Explains how the subject influenced the world while he or she lived
- Researches the cultural and historical context of the subject's life
- Examines the effect that the subject has had on the modern world
- Supplements information from the biography with independent research
- Organizes the analysis in a logical, effective manner
- Uses correct spelling, grammar, and punctuation
- Cites all sources used in the analysis

Germs and Disease

The scientific approach that harnessed first steam and then electricity in the 1700s and 1800s led to great advances in medical understanding. Before the middle of the 1800s, most people blamed "evil spirits" or "bad air" for the spread of disease. As early as 1546, however, the Italian physician Girolamo Fracastoro had suggested that germs are the cause of disease. Much later, in 1840, German pathologist Jacob Henle put forward the idea that infection is caused by parasitic organisms. This so-called "germ theory" of disease was later proposed independently by French chemist Louis Pasteur. In 1877, German bacteriologist Robert Koch showed that bacteria could be stained to make them easier to study under a microscope.

Classifying Bacteria

Seven years later, the Danish physician Hans Gram used this idea as the basis for a means of classifying bacteria. Since then, bacteria have been labeled either Gram-positive or Gram-negative, depending on their capacity to absorb a special stain. Bacteriologists also classify bacteria according to their shapes. Coccus bacteria are round, bacillus are oval shaped, spirochete have the shape of a spiral, and so on.

Once biologists knew what bacteria looked like, the hunt was on to find more, even though scientists who handled cultures of infectious diseases often put themselves at risk. Results came quite quickly. In 1880, German bacteriologist Karl Eberth found the bacillus that causes typhoid. In 1882, German bacteriologist Robert Koch found the bacterium that causes tuberculosis, and in the same year, German bacteriologists Friedrich Löffler and Wilhelm Schütz identified the cause of the animal disease glanders. In 1897, the Japanese bacteriologist Kiyoshi Shiga found the cause of endemic dysentery, a serious stomach problem.

Louis Pasteur used his knowledge of bacteria to develop pasteurization, a way of preventing milk from turning sour.

Viruses

Viruses are too small to be trapped by a filter that retains bacteria. For this reason, they evaded discovery until the very end of the nineteenth century. Even so, no one actually saw a virus until after the invention of the electron microscope in the late 1930s. These microorganisms turned out to have various shapes, and to consist of an outer "container" of protein holding a molecule of either deoxyribonucleic acid (DNA), or ribonucleic acid (RNA). Various structures may project from the outer surface. Viruses cannot multiply outside a living cell, but once they force their way into a cell, they take it over and make it rapidly reproduce more virus particles. The particles break out, and quickly invade other cells. Shown below are an adenovirus (A) that causes acute respiratory disorders, a bacteriophage (B) that attacks bacteria, and HIV (human immune deficiency virus), which causes AIDS (C).

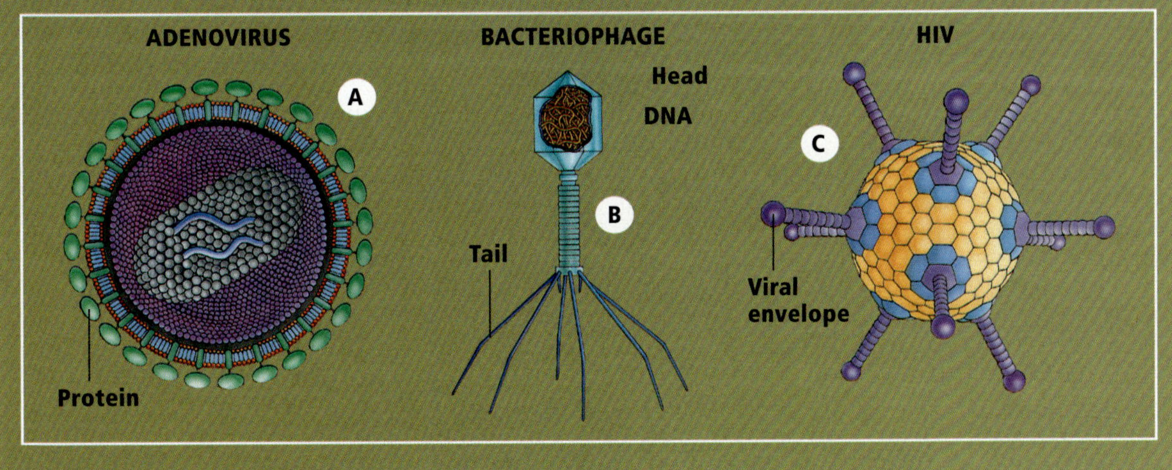

Harmful Microorganisms

Bacteria are not the only parasitic microorganisms to cause human diseases. Protozoans, for example, include the trypanosomes that cause sleeping sickness and Chagas' disease. They also include the amebas that result in amebic dysentery, and the Plasmodium parasite responsible for malaria. Some microscopic fungi produce diseases of the skin or lungs. Most of these microorganisms were tracked down by nineteenth-century microbiologists.

Fighting Viruses

In 1897, Dutch microbiologist Martinus Beijerinck showed that the microorganism causing tobacco mosaic disease escapes through a filter that traps bacteria. He had discovered the first virus. Since then, viruses have been found to be responsible for many diseases. As bacteriologists found the bacteria that cause diseases, they developed **vaccines** against them that gave people immunity. Vaccines for virus diseases proved more difficult, but now exist for nearly all disorders.

ACTIVITIES

Transparency

Viruses

Examine the diagram showing different viruses.

1. Describe how scientists were able to recognize the presence of viruses even though they could not see them before the invention of the electron microscope. Why can viruses not multiply outside a living cell?
2. Summarize the structure of a virus. Explain the methods whereby scientists can draw diagrams such as these of viruses.

Weblink

The History of Germ Theory

Review this weblink on the two scientists who proved that disease was created by micro-organisms.

1. Rather than Hippocrates' "bad air," describe what might cause disease in swampy regions. What do we now call the substance Pasteur described as "ferment?"
2. Describe how Koch may have grown anthrax bacteria in his laboratory. Explain what process might Koch have used to isolate tuberculosis bacteria.

RUBRIC

Create a Scientific Drawing

Create a scientific drawing of a carburetor. An exemplary scientific drawing will meet the following criteria:

- Includes a descriptive an accurate title
- The drawing(s) realistically depicts the object(s)
- The drawing only includes features that were actually observed
- Relevant details such as size, colors, textures, shapes, and relationships to surroundings are included
- Multiple perspectives are drawn to provide the viewer with a complete picture
- All parts of the scientific drawing are clearly labeled with the correct terms
- A written explanation of the drawing shows what is included in the drawing
- A key or legend is provided
- An appropriate size and scale is chosen for the drawing so that the details are easily recognized

The Internal Combustion Engine

In a steam engine, combustion of the fuel in order to boil water and make steam takes place outside the engine mechanism itself. It is an example of an external combustion engine. An engine is much more efficient if the fuel burns inside the cylinder. This happens in an internal combustion engine.

Gas Engine

When invented: 1876

Where invented: Cologne, Germany

Inventor: Nikolaus Otto

Fuel: Coal gas

Advantages: First four-stroke engine, quiet operation

Drawbacks: Too large for practical uses in transportation and requires large amounts of coal

Gasoline Engine

When invented: 1885

Where invented: Germany

Inventors: Karl Benz, Gottleib Daimler, Wilhelm Maybach

Fuel: Liquid gasoline

Advantages: Small and light, so suitable for automobiles

Drawbacks: Complicated engineering leads to breakdown, highly flammable fuel

The Belgian engineer Étienne Lenoir built an internal combustion engine in 1859. Coal gas and air were sucked into the cylinder by a piston and ignited, forcing the piston to the end of its stroke. As the piston moved back, gas and air were sucked in on the other side of it, and the process was repeated.

Diesel Engine

When invented: 1893

Where invented: Berlin, Germany

Inventor: Rudolf Diesel

Fuel: Diesel fuel

Advantages: Uses less refined fuel than gasoline engines, and burns fuel more efficiently

Drawbacks: Heavy exhaust emissions

Rotary Engine

When invented: 1929 (built 1957)

Where invented: Neckarsulm, Germany

Inventor: Felix Wankel

Fuel: Liquid gasoline

Advantages: Smoother and more compact than piston engines, rotary motion easily adaptable to many applications

Drawbacks: Slow combustion, poor fuel efficiency, high emissions

ACTIVITIES

More

The Internal Combustion Engine
Review the four major types of engine: gas engine, gasoline engine, diesel engine, rotary engine.

1. Describe the importance of the carburetor in the gasoline engine. Compare Benz's automobile engine with that of Otto. Why was Benz's better?
2. Summarize the differences between a gasoline engine and a diesel engine. Why are governments nowadays considering phasing out diesel engines?

RUBRIC

Answer a Scientific Question

Research the best metals for creating a simple voltaic pile and carry out a scientific investigation or experiment to discover whether Volta's use of copper or silver and zinc are the best to use. Write a report on your investigation. An exemplary report will meet the following criteria:

- The problem is written in the form of a question with a question mark at the end
- The hypothesis is written as a guess or explanation to the answer of the problem
- The hypothesis is written in a complete sentence. (I think ..., I hypothesize ..., If.. then...)
- The variable and controls are clearly identified
- Procedure steps are in numbered order
- Procedure steps show what to measure and where to record the data
- Procedure steps are written in complete sentences
- The data is organized in a data table
- The experiment or investigation includes more then one trial
- All numbers have labels (cm., ml., g.)
- All calculations complete
- Conclusion written in complete sentences
- Conclusion states whether your hypothesis was right or wrong
- Conclusion answers the question written in the problem

Sources of Electricity

In 1791, Italian physician Luigi Galvani reported what he called "animal electricity." While dissecting a dead frog, he found that the animal's muscles twitched when he touched them with two different metals. Then, in 1800, Count Alessandro Volta, an Italian physicist, replaced the animal tissue with a disk of cardboard soaked in salt solution. He put a piece of either copper or silver on one side, and a piece of zinc on the other side. Wires connected to the metal plates carried an electric current. Volta found he could obtain higher voltages by making a stack of such disks to form what became known as a voltaic pile. This was the first true battery.

Alessandro Volta demonstrated his battery widely, including to Emperor Napoleon in France.

Improving the System

Today, scientists call such a battery a primary cell. The pieces of metal are called electrodes, and the solution between them is an **electrolyte**. In 1836, English chemist John Daniell produced a primary cell. It had a zinc rod electrode dipped in dilute sulfuric acid, contained in an earthenware pot. He immersed the pot in a copper container, which acted as the other electrode, containing copper sulfate solution. An electric current flowed from the copper, which was the positive electrode, or **anode**, to the zinc, which formed the negative electrode, or cathode. The Daniell's cell gives a steadier current than Volta's cell. The Leclanché cell, a battery invented in 1866 by French engineer Georges Leclanché, also has a zinc cathode.

Primary and Secondary Cells

A primary cell, such as the dry battery for a flashlight, can be used only until its chemicals run out, when it has to be thrown away. In this type of cell, the electrolyte is a paste of ammonium chloride and gum. The zinc cathode forms the case of the battery, and manganese dioxide and carbon surround the central carbon anode. A secondary cell, or accumulator, can be recharged and reused. It has lead and lead-oxide electrodes in a sulfuric-acid electrolyte. When it is in use, sulfate ions react with the lead cathode to produce lead sulfate and release electrons. At the anode, **hydrogen** ions from the acid and sulfate ions react with the lead oxide to produce lead sulfate and water. The reactions produce about 2 volts. To recharge the accumulator, current from an outside source is passed through the battery in the opposite direction. This has the effect of reversing the reactions at the electrodes, reforming lead and lead oxide. The accumulator is then ready for use again. Automobiles use batteries of this type.

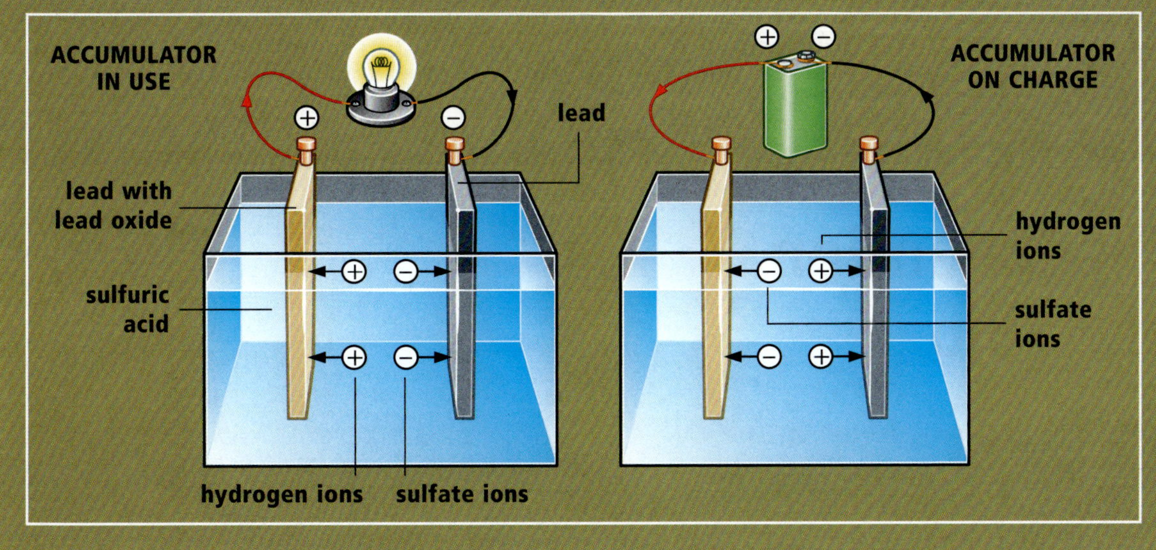

The anode is a carbon rod surrounded by manganese dioxide. Today's dry battery has the same system, using a zinc case with a paste of ammonium chloride around a carbon rod surrounded by manganese dioxide.

Other Metals

German chemist Robert Bunsen also made a zinc–carbon primary cell using acid electrolytes. The cadmium cell, invented in 1893 by U.S. engineer Edward Weston, produces 1.0186 volts. In 1908, the cadmium cell's output became a standard of voltage. The Weston standard cell has mercury and a cadmium–mercury mixture as its electrodes, with cadmium sulfate solution as its electrolyte. The Clark standard cell, invented by English engineer Josiah Clark in 1872, uses zinc instead of cadmium.

ACTIVITIES

Transparency

Primary and Secondary Cells

Examine the diagram of an accumulator.

1. Describe the advantages of an accumulator over a dry battery cell. Why is an accumulator not practical for most household applications?
2. Describe the properties of an electrolyte. Why is the element zinc so important in the activity of automobile batteries?

Weblink

Alessandro Volta's Experiments

Review the weblink about this important scientific debate.

1. Summarize the working parts of the battery, or "pile", that Volta created. Why did this battery create electricity?
2. Describe some of the immediate applications of Volta's invention for scientific progress. Why is Galvani also considered a scientific pioneer?

Although Guglielmo Marconi had little scientific training, he won the Nobel Prize in Physics in 1909.

The Invention of Radio

Radio has its origins in the late nineteenth century. Danish physicist Hans Ørsted had realized that electricity and magnetism were both part of a phenomenon called electromagnetism. In 1864, physicist James Clerk Maxwell showed that energy could be transmitted as an electromagnetic wave at the speed of light. In 1888, the German physicist Heinrich Hertz produced electromagnetic waves by generating large electrical sparks that jumped between two metal spheres. Hertz and Maxwell had laid the foundations for "wireless telegraphy," or radio.

The "Coherer"

In 1890, French physicist Édouard Branly devised a way of detecting radio waves. This "coherer" was a sealed glass tube containing iron filings and an electrode at each end. When radio waves are present, the filings stick together, or cohere, and conduct electricity as part of a circuit. English physicist Oliver Lodge improved the coherer in 1894, and used it to send Morse code messages a distance of 490 feet (150 m). Russian physicist Aleksandr Popov conducted similar experiments a year later.

Birth of Radiotelegraphy

The early development of radio is credited largely to the Italian engineer, Guglielmo Marconi. He began experimenting with radio in 1894.

In 1895, Marconi used radio to transmit telegraph signals more than a mile (1.6 km). The invention became known as radiotelegraphy. On December 12, 1901, Marconi sent a Morse code message from Cornwall in southwestern England to Newfoundland in Canada.

Voices on the Radio

Carrying the voice by radio is called radiotelephony. It was pioneered by U.S. electrical engineer Reginald Fessenden, who invented modulation. In this process, a transmitter sends out a continuous carrier wave. The wave's **amplitude**, or strength, is varied, or modulated, by sound signals from a microphone. Fessenden demonstrated AM, or amplitude modulation, in 1903. By 1906, he could transmit speech and music.

Picking Up the Signal

The new system needed a better detector. This came in the form of an improved crystal detector, produced by U.S. electrical engineer Greenleaf Pickard in 1906. It converted the incoming signal from alternating current to direct current. The detector connected to the radio circuit by a thin wire, which was nicknamed "cat's whisker." English engineer John Fleming had invented a better system in 1904. This was a two-electrode **vacuum tube** called a diode. Two years later, U.S. engineer Lee De Forest added a third electrode to make the triode vacuum tube, which could boost weak radio signals. With the aid of the new devices, radio engineers could build better circuits for transmitters and receivers.

Lee De Forest is known as the "father of the transistor."

In 1917, Marconi began making VHF, or very high frequency, transmissions. By 1924, he was also sending speech signals from England to Australia using short-wave radio. Vacuum tubes have largely been replaced in radios now by much smaller transistors, invented by the Bell Laboratories, New Jersey, in 1948.

2,200 MILES
(3,540 KM)
FIRST MESSAGE
The distance covered by Marconi's first long-distance Morse Code message from Cornwall to Canada.

1,000
LISTENERS
About 1,000 Americans listened to the first radio broadcast, announcing the results of the presidential election in November 1920.

ACTIVITIES

Video

Guglielmo Marconi Wireless Telegraphy
Review this video on Marconi's researches.

1. Describe the breakthrough of Heinrich Hertz on electromagnetic waves. Why did the example of light waves help in the invention of radio?
2. Explain the importance of earthing in Marconi's researches. Describe the activity of electrons in radio waves.

Weblink

Vacuum Tubes
Examine the weblink on vacuum tubes.

1. Summarize thermionic emission. Why does the vacuum help in the process of boosting radio signals?
2. Explain why the triode system is more effective at amplifying signals than the diode set up. Summarize the advantages of transistors over triode vacuum tubes.

Elusive Electrons

Until the late nineteenth century, many unanswered questions remained about the nature of electricity. These questions would be answered thanks to the invention of the vacuum pump, which allowed scientists to remove air from a piece of apparatus. One of the first people to use it was the German glassblower Heinrich Geissler. In about 1850, he sealed metal plates inside a glass vacuum tube containing traces of a gas such as neon or argon. He joined the plates to a source of electricity, which then created lighting effects as the gas glowed in the container. Geissler tubes became a popular novelty, but they were also used for serious experiments by two German physicists, Julius Plücker in 1859, and Johann Hittorf in 1869. They maintained that the light resulted from "rays" that left the negatively charged plate, or cathode, of the Geissler tube and traveled in straight lines to the anode. This theory was confirmed in 1879 by English physicist William Crookes, who also suggested that the "rays" might be particles. Sixteen years later, French physicist Jean Perrin deflected these so-called cathode rays using magnetic and electric fields. Perrin proved that the rays are made up of negative electric charges.

Physicists such as Ernest Rutherford figured out the nature of electricity and the role of electrons over about 30 years.

Electrons and Electricity

Ernest Rutherford proposed a model of the structure of the atom in which electrons orbit a central nucleus. In some elements, however, electrons tend to wander away from their atomic nuclei to form a "sea" of free electrons. This happens particularly in metals, such as copper. If such a metal is used to create a wire or cable, and a voltage is applied to it, these free electrons move and become an electric current flowing along the cable. The fewer free electrons a metal has, the more resistant the metal is to conducting electricity.

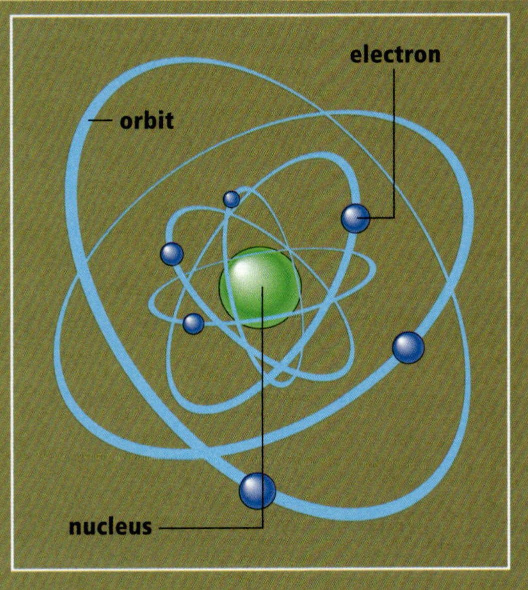

The scene was set for the experiments of the English physicist Joseph John Thomson, known as "J.J." Thomson graduated from Cambridge University in 1880. He went to work in the famous Cavendish Laboratory, and became its professor in 1884.

Subatomic "Corpuscles"

Thomson deflected cathode rays with electric and magnetic fields. He showed that they travel more slowly than light waves. He also figured out that the ratio of their charge to their mass was 1,000 times smaller than for a hydrogen ion, the smallest charged atom. Thomson deduced that cathode rays consist of minute, negatively charged particles. He announced the discovery of these subatomic particles, which he called "corpuscles," in 1897. Thomson later found that they have a mass about one two-thousandth of the mass of a hydrogen atom. The' existence of the particles had been predicted in 1874 by Irish physicist George Stoney, who named them "electrons." The electron turned out to be the unit responsible for electrostatic charges. A flow of electrons along a **conductor** forms an electric current. Electrons are fundamental to all atoms.

Thomson's later studies led in 1912 to him finding a way of separating charged particles. This helped Francis Aston to develop the mass spectrograph in 1919. The device identifies the elements in a substance. When Thomson retired in 1919, he was succeeded by his former assistant, New Zealand-born physicist Ernest Rutherford. Rutherford eventually proposed a structure for the atom that included the atomic nucleus.

ACTIVITIES

Transparency

Electrons and Electricity

Examine the diagram on electrons.

1. Are electrons actual particles or are they better understood as moving electrical charges? Describe metals other than copper that produce free electrons.
2. Why are metals that conduct electricity easily not good for conducting electricity in the microchips that power computers? What types of material are better in microchips?

Weblink

Cathode Rays: Experiments of J.J. Thomson

Review the weblink on J.J. Thomson's experiments.

1. Why does electricity create a fluorescent glow in a cathode ray tube? Why could early researchers not decide whether cathode rays were waves or particles?
2. Summarize how Thomson discovered that cathode rays carried a negative charge. Why did this discovery form the basis of Rutherford's description of the structure of the atom?

RUBRIC

Researching for a Writing Assignment

Students will complete a thorough research process to prepare for a writing assignment on the invention of the automobile, and organize their research in a logical manner that supports their writing. An exemplary research process will meet the following criteria:

- Creates a goal for the research, based on the topic and working thesis
- Creates specific, thoughtful, and inventive research questions that are relevant to the topic of the writing assignment
- Produces a list of categories, key words, and related ideas to effectively assist in researching
- Uses high-quality sources that pertain to the topic and come in a variety of formats, such as books, journals, primary sources, websites, and databases
- Uses sources that provide balanced research and various perspectives of the topic in question
- Takes notes to highlight the key facts and ideas in order to answer all research questions
- Extracts relevant, detailed information from the sources
- Writes notes in the student's own words
- Organizes the research notes in a clear and concise manner
- Analyzes the information and produces ideas and points to support the working thesis
- Uses an effective and suitable format to present all research
- Properly cites all sources used
- Uses quotations properly and ethically

Early Automobiles

The automobile was the result of a long period of trial and error in the quest for a motorized road vehicle. The early machines had to use a steam engine, the only motive power available at the time. Motor travel was revolutionized by the internal combustion engine, fueled first by gasoline and later also by diesel. Inventors around the world contributed to the evolution of the modern motor car in the late 1800s and early 1900s.

DETROIT, MICHIGAN

The U.S. inventor Henry Ford began making cars in Detroit in 1903. In 1908, he introduced the popular Model T Ford, which became the first mass-ownership car. In 1913, he built the world's first automated production line in a plant at Highland Park, Detroit. This enabled cars to be built quickly and more cheaply, which allowed more people to afford them.

LEGEND

- Land
- Ocean
- Car manufacturers
- Mannheim, Germany
- Le Mans, France
- Detroit, United States
- Springfield, United States

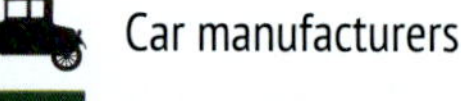

SPRINGFIELD, MASSACHUSETTS

In 1893, the brothers Charles and Frank Duryea built the first gasoline-engine car in the United States, the Duryea Motor Wagon. Two years later, they founded the Duryea Motor Wagon Company at Springfield, where they built the first 10 cars ever to be sold in the United States.

LE MANS, FRANCE

In 1873, French engineer Amédée Bollée built a 12-seater steam carriage called *L'Obéissante*, or "the Obedient One," at his workshop in Le Mans near Paris, La Mancelle. Five years later, he built "The Young Lady from Le Mans." It had a front-mounted engine driving the rear wheels, and could travel at up to 25 miles per hour (40 km/h).

MANNHEIM, GERMANY

Like his countryman and contemporary, Gottleib Daimler, German engineer Karl Benz realized that the gasoline engine offered a more promising means to power a vehicle than steam. He built his first car, a three-wheeler called the Motorwagen, in Mannheim in 1885. It had a 1-**horsepower** engine and a maximum speed of 8 miles per hour (13 km/h).

ACTIVITIES

Google Maps

Early Automobiles

Examine the map of the major automobile manufacturing countries.

1. Why are the early automobile centers in the most industrialized parts of the world? Describe the infrastructure that automobiles require for movement, refueling, etc.
2. Describe how gasoline and diesel fuel for automobiles was made from crude oil. Summarize the military application of automobiles up to 1914.

Airships

The first hot-air balloon flew in 1783. Without a power source, however, balloons were at the mercy of the winds. The advantages of a controllable balloon were clear. By the late 1800s, every military power that could afford it was rushing to build a "ship of the air."

To make a balloon steerable, it needed to have a motor and a rudder. The Frenchman Henri Giffard created the first such aircraft in 1852. Now known as an airship, the aircraft was originally called by the French name "dirigible," meaning "steerable." Giffard's craft consisted of a long, cigar-shaped envelope, or gasbag, containing hydrogen. Ropes supported a cabin, or gondola, that carried the pilot and engine. The envelope kept its shape because of the pressure of the gas inside.

Lack of Power

Giffard's craft was powered by a steam engine that turned a propeller. However, the weight of this engine meant that a great deal of gas was needed to lift the ship off the ground. A rudder behind the gondola steered the craft. The gondola was suspended well below the gasbag in case sparks from the engine ignited the hydrogen.

Electricity and Gasoline

Although Giffard's dirigible was an improvement on normal balloons, a more powerful engine was needed to fly in anything other than a light breeze. In 1883, French brothers Albert and Gaston Tissandier powered a dirigible with an electric motor. Battery motors became popular, but they were heavy. In 1872, however, German engineer Paul Haenlein had fitted the much lighter, internal-combustion engine to a dirigible.

During World War I, major cities such as London used large searchlights to look out for Zeppelins.

To save even more weight, Haenlein used hydrogen from the gasbag to power the engine. Inventors began increasingly to use gasoline engines to power airships.

Semirigid and Rigid Frames

In 1898, a semirigid airship appeared. Metal frames in the nose and rear were connected by a wooden lattice keel. The first rigid airship, which had an internal metal framework, was built by Austrian inventor David Schwartz in 1897. Aluminum was now the favored metal for construction. It was used by German engineer Count Ferdinand von Zeppelin for his first airship, the LZ-1, in 1900. The first truly successful zeppelin was the LZ-4 of 1908. At the time, the LZ-4 was the largest airship in the skies, at 446 feet (136 m) long. On July 4, 1908, the LZ-4 traveled at 40 miles per hour (60 km/h) for 12 hours over Switzerland.

The 486-foot (148-m) *Deutschland* inaugurated the world's first commercial airline in 1910. It was followed by *Graf Zeppelin*, a 771-foot (235-m) airship that could carry passengers across the Atlantic Ocean at speeds of up to 81 miles per hour (130 km/h). The outbreak of World War I in 1914 proved to be the real spur to airship construction. Germany led the world, constructing 88 military airships between 1914 and 1918. London was the first city to be attacked from the air, when a group of "zeppelins" made a nighttime raid on Britain's capital in May 1915.

Crash of the Hindenburg

After World War I, the airship was increasingly replaced by airplanes. Airships developed a reputation for being dangerous. Although hydrogen is the lightest of all gases, it is also one of the most flammable. Of the five airships built between 1920 and 1933 by the U.S. Navy, three crashed. In 1930, the British airship *R101* crashed in France on its way to India. Of the 54 people on board, 48 died. In 1936, the German airship *Hindenburg* made its first flight. Later that same year, it began regular transatlantic crossings. In 1937, when the *Hindenburg* was nearing its mooring at Lakehurst, New Jersey, its hydrogen caught fire and the airship exploded. A total of 36 people onboard died. Such disasters marked the end of the age of the airship.

ACTIVITIES

First Hand

Herb Morrison Radio Broadcast *Hindenburg* Crash, 1937

Examine this transcript of the most famous airship disaster.

1. Why was the reporter so clearly astounded by the suddenness of the crash of the *Hindenburg* when there had been other airship crashes previously? Compare the loss of life in the *Hindenburg* disaster with the loss of life when the *Titanic* sank.
2. Explain why U.S. government policy contributed to the crash of the *Hindenburg*. Describe contemporary theories of the cause of the crash.

Weblink

All About Airships

Review this website about lighter- than-air machines.

1. Describe how the internal combustion engine changed airship design. Why was a rigid frame so important in Zeppelin design?
2. Explain the military applications of airships during World War I. What was the main weakness of airships as a military technology?

RUBRIC

Sketch a Design Solution

As a group, look at the problem of creating an aircraft that can fly for 20 yards (18 meters). Brainstorm possible solutions and select the best design solution. Make a sketch of a model or prototype. An exemplary project will meet the following criteria:

- The problem is defined in detail
- All constraints are listed
- Possible solutions from the brainstorming session are listed
- Two or three ideas are selected from brainstormed list
- Sketches are created for the selected idea
- Sketches are labeled with dimensions and materials for each component
- Detailed list of materials is included
- Detailed procedures are included
- Hypothesis following an "if.., then..." format is developed for the design
- Strengths of the design are listed
- Weaknesses of the design or compromises of the design are listed
- The chosen design effectively addresses the identified problem
- Modifications to the design are documented
- Presentation is well-organized
- Presentation is clearly communicated visually with appropriate data, sketches, graphs or pictures
- Presentation includes contributions from all team members

Pioneers of Flight

Even before the invention of lighter-than-air flying machines, such as balloons, people wanted to take to the air like birds. The artist and inventor Leonardo da Vinci drew a flying machine in about 1500. No such machine could ever have flown, because it depended on human muscle power for propulsion.

George Cayley

Full name: Sir George Cayley

Born: 1773, Yorkshire, United Kingdom

Died: 1857, Yorkshire, United Kingdom

Nationality: English

Profession: Politician, engineer, aviator

Main contribution: Glider of 1853 was the first heavier-than-air machine to carry a human passenger

Otto Lilienthal

Full name: Karl Wilhelm Otto Lilienthal

Born: 1848, Pomerania

Died: 1896, Berlin, Germany

Nationality: German

Profession: Engineer

Main contribution: Well-documented series of glider flights made powered flight a more realistic possibility

ACTIVITIES

The first heavier-than-air machines to fly were kites, invented by the Chinese in about 1000 BC. In the late nineteenth century, human-carrying kites were built, including one designed for military use by English soldier Baden Baden-Powell. Real progress only began when people began experimenting with gliders.

Samuel Langley

Full name: Samuel Pierpoint Langley

Born: 1834, Roxbury, MA, United States

Died: 1906, Aiken, SC, United States

Nationality: American

Profession: Astronomer, physicist

Main contribution: Designed successful heavier-than-air, steam-powered model airplanes in the 1890s

The Wright Brothers

Full names: Orville and Wilbur Wright

Born: 1871, Dayton OH (Orville), 1867 Millville IN (Wilbur), United States

Died: 1948, Dayton OH (Orville), 1912, Dayton, OH (Wilbur), United States

Nationality: American

Profession: Bicycle repairers, engineers, inventors, and aviators

Main contribution: First controlled, sustained, heavier-than-air flight in 1903

More

Pioneers of Flight

Review the four major innovators in the history of flight: George Cayley, Otto Lilienthal, Samuel Langley, and the Wright Brothers.

1. Why was the biplane the first successful glider technology? Why was the bicycle more important than bird flight as a basis for early flying machines?
2. Explain the importance of aluminum in the early flights of the Wright brothers. Describe how the wind tunnel they created was crucial to the Wright brothers' success.

Capturing Sound

The age of sound recording arrived in 1877. The U.S. inventor Thomas Alva Edison launched his mechanical phonograph cylinder. It was the first commercially available machine that could capture sound and then play it back.

Best known for developing the telephone, Alexander Graham Bell developed an interest in sound through his work with deaf people. He wanted to improve the sound quality of Edison's phonograph, and in 1886, he took out a patent on his "graphophone." In Bell's machine, a needle vibrated from side to side in response to sound waves. It made indentations on a tinfoil drum.

A year later, the German inventor Emile Berliner demonstrated his own gramophone. This machine recorded sound in grooves on a disk of zinc covered in wax. Berliner produced a metal mold of a master disk and realized he could press cheap copies. By 1901, Berliner's Victor Talking Machine Company had a catalog of more than 5,000 recordings for the gramophone. The mass production of disks meant that people could hear their favorite artists in their own homes.

Magnetic Recordings

Other inventors set out to capture sound using magnetism and electricity. In 1878, the American Oberlin Smith recorded the electrical signals made by a telephone onto a steel wire. After failing to gain investment, in 1888, Smith donated his ideas to the public by publishing them in a magazine.

Ten years later, Danish physicist Valdeman Poulsen created the first dictation and answering machine. This telegraphone recorded messages onto a steel wire, which was coiled around a cylinder that rotated under an electromagnet connected to a telephone earpiece. The invention was not popular.

The Berliner gramophone used a hand-turned crank to rotate a wax-covered disk on a turntable, with an ear horn linked to a needle.

In 1888, Oberlin Smith put forward the idea that strips of fabric covered with iron filings could be used to record sounds. However, it was not until 50 years later that Austro-German scientist Fritz Pfleumer patented the first magnetic recording tape, a paper strip coated with a magnetizable steel layer. The German electrical company AEG bought the patent and developed the idea by coating plastic tape with iron-oxide powder. In 1935, AEG demonstrated its new recording machine, the magnetophon, which was the first reel-to-reel tape recorder. These older tape recorders used yards of tape. Gradually, however, tapes became shorter. In 1964, the Dutch company Philips developed the cassette tape. This format, which was only 4 inches (10 cm) long, became very popular.

Improving Sound Quality

By the 1920s, sound quality had become very important. In 1925, Bell Laboratories perfected a system of recording sound electrically. By converting sound into electric current, they could use smaller microphones. Electrical microphones enabled all of the recording to be heard, whereas in mechanical recordings the louder sounds always came out best. The microphone allowed softer sounds, such as those produced by violins and harps, to be recorded and clearly heard. The first stereo records were eventually introduced in 1958, and were made by recording two channels of sound to reproduce the acoustic of a live concert hall.

Edison's Phonograph

Thomas Alva Edison based the development of his phonograph on experiments that had been carried out in the 1850s. Scientists interested in sound attached a flexible diaphragm, or thin disk or cone, to a fine needle that rested against a moving glass plate covered in soot. Sound made the diaphragm vibrate, causing the needle to trace wavy lines in the soot. This showed that sound travels in waves.

Edison attached a speaker horn to a needle that rested on a tinfoil drum. A voice was recorded by turning the drum by hand while the speaker spoke into the speaker horn. The needle made a series of tiny indentations in the tinfoil that represented the sound waves. In order to play the sound back, the needle was replaced with a bristle. As the drum was rotated, the bristles picked up the indentations and reproduced the sound waves.

Document

Edison's Phonograph Patent Application

Examine Edison's patent application.

1. Why does the beginning of the patent mention the human voice but not music? What was the role of clockwork in Edison's patent application?
2. Describe what material would be best for the diaphragm. What would be the disadvantages of reproducing the tinfoil indentations using the "plaster of Paris" method? Why did shellac become the substance used to make gramophone records?

Weblink

A Brief History of Recording to ca. 1950

Review the website dealing with the early history of recorded sound.

1. Why was tinfoil a good substance to wrap around the cylindrical drum? What were the advantages of a wax cylinder over tinfoil?
2. Describe another technology that made use of lampblack to reproduce sound waves in the late 1800s. Why were 12-inch discs better than 7-inch discs for reproducing sound on early gramophones?

RUBRIC

You Decide

Research the topic of the dangers of plastics online and present a scientific argument that explains whether you believe that plastics should be banned. An exemplary scientific argument will meet the following criteria"

- Provides background on the topic within the introduction
- Introduction is logical and provides accurate scientific information
- Alternative opinions are explained, and are related to the controversy of the topic
- Research is explained, including critiques of websites
- Scientific information is accurate. All relevant pieces of evidence are analyzed.
- Well-supported stance is justified by analysis
- Explanation of stance incorporates and explains personal opinions, as well as reflects on opinions that changed throughout the research process
- Usefulness and credibility of websites is discussed
- More than four websites are consulted, and sources are properly cited
- Free of grammatical and spelling errors

Plastics

Plastics are synthetic materials that can be molded into a variety of shapes, usually by applying heat or pressure. Cheaper than many other materials, plastics have numerous uses in the home, in industry, and in medicine. Before the invention of synthetic plastics in the mid-1800s, many objects were made from natural materials that already had plastic-like properties. Combs and other intricately shaped objects were made from carved animal horn, for example. Gutta-percha, a tree gum from Malaysia, was used to manufacture electrical equipment and cables, and shellac, a hard material secreted by some insects, was used to mold records.

Nitrocellulose, which is produced by dipping cotton into a mixture of nitric and sulfuric acids, formed the basis of the first plastics. In 1855, the British chemist Alexander Parkes created a flexible, durable material called Parkesine. It was made from a mixture of nitrocellulose, alcohol, camphor, and vegetable oils.

Celluloid

In the United States, John Wesley Hyatt was looking for a cheap substitute for ivory to make billiard balls. After he heard about Parkes's work, Hyatt developed a new plastic called celluloid, and in 1872, he set up a company to manufacture the substance. Celluloid was used for making shirt collars and cuffs, knife handles, photographic films, and billiard balls.

Bakelite was easy to mold into attractive shapes for appliances.

Making Polymers

Polymers are giant molecules made up of many smaller parts, called monomers, joined in a long chain. Natural polymers include lignin, the main component of wood, and collagen, the substance that forms hair and fingernails. Synthetic polymers, or plastics, are among the most useful and widespread of modern materials. By altering the structure of the building blocks, and the conditions under which they react, chemists can make polymers with properties to suit particular needs, from clothing to aircraft parts. A polythene molecule is a straight chain of between 1,000 and 5,000 ethene molecules that are passed through a catalyst and form new bonds with polymer molecules.

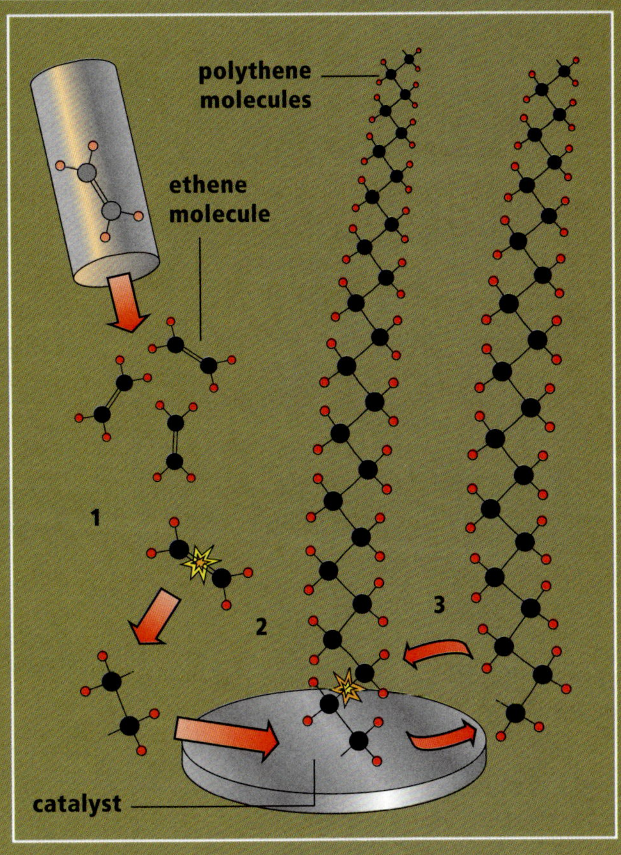

ACTIVITIES

Transparency

Making Polymers

Examine the diagram about the making of polymers.

1. Compare the chain of a polythene molecule with that of a collagen molecule. Explain the role of the catalyst in creating polythene.
2. Explain how chemists would make a polymer that was flexible, and compare this with how they would make a polymer that was stronger and more rigid. Why are crosslinks a valuable property of thermoplastics?

Weblink

The History and Future of Plastics

Review the website on the story of how plastics were invented.

1. Why is carbon so important in making modern plastics? How was cellulose used by John Wesley Hyatt in his celluloid?
2. Explain some of the military applications of plastic that led to the expansion of the plastics industry during World War II. Summarize the main disadvantages with the widespread use of plastics in the twenty-first century.

Bakelite

The first truly synthetic plastic was Bakelite, which first went on sale in the United States in 1909. The Belgian chemist Leo Hendrik Baekeland came up with the substance while he was searching for a synthetic alternative to rubber, which tended to dry out and crack after frequent use. Made from phenol and formaldehyde, Bakelite is tough and easy to produce. The dark-colored plastic was shaped and used in many household appliances, such as radios and TV sets. Bakelite also became a common insulator in electrical equipment.

Synthetic Garments

In 1883, Joseph Swan patented a process to produce thin nitrocellulose filaments. French chemist Count Hilaire de Chardonnet developed these fibers into rayon for use in clothing in 1935. In 1928, Wallace Hume Carothers began investigating the production of polymers, which are synthetic plastics formed by joining molecules into long chains. After many tests, he produced a fiber named 66-polyamide, now known as nylon, which was elastic, tough, and water resistant. In 1940, the first nylon stockings appeared in stores.

Timeline of Science Discoveries

The nineteenth and early twentieth centuries saw many discoveries being made around the world. These are some of the most important breakthroughs. They cover a wide range of fields of science.

	1820–1830	1830–1840	1840–1850	1850–1860	1860–1870
Technology	**1826** French chemist Joseph Niépce takes the first photograph. **1829** The English engineer George Stephenson builds *The Rocket* steam locomotive.	**1838** U.S. inventor Samuel Morse demonstrates a single-wire electric telegraph over a 10-mile (16-km) circuit.	**1844** Samuel Morse sends the first message on a telegraph line, from Washington, D.C., to Baltimore. **1848** English inventor John Stringfellow builds a model steam-driven airplane.	**1853** English inventor George Cayley constructs a glider capable of carrying a person. **1856** Henry Bessemer develops the Bessemer converter for making steel out of iron.	**1863** French chemist Louis Pasteur introduces pasteurization, a process that kills bacteria in food. **1869** The first transcontinental railroad is completed in the United States.
Biology and Medicine	**1827** U.S. artist John James Audubon publishes the first part of *Birds of America.* **1828** Estonian naturalist Karl von Baer founds embryology, the study of embryos.	**1831** Scottish botanist Robert Brown describes the nucleus of a cell, specifically a plant cell.	**1840** Frenchman Jean Boussingault identifies nitrates in the soil as a source of nitrogen for plants. **1842** U.S. surgeon Crawford Long uses ether as an anesthetic.	**1859** English naturalist Charles Darwin publishes *On the Origin of Species*, the book in which he puts forward his theory of evolution.	**1865** Austrian monk Gregor Mendel outlines his two laws of inheritance.
Physical Sciences	**1827** German Georg Ohm publishes Ohm's law, which states that the voltage across a conductor divided by the current flowing through it is a constant, called the resistance.	**1834** English scientist Michael Faraday formulates laws of electrolysis, the process by which an electrical current running through a liquid causes chemical reactions at the electrodes.	**1845** The French physicists Armand Fizeau and Léon Foucault take detailed photographs of the Sun.	**1854** U.S. chemist David Alter uses atomic spectra, given off by heated elements, for chemical analysis. **1855** English chemist Alexander Parkes develops the first celluloid.	**1869** Russian chemist Dmitri Mendeleev compiles the first Periodic Table of the Elements.

1870–1880	1880–1890	1890–1900	1900–1905	1905–1910
1876 Scottish-born U.S. engineer Alexander Graham Bell patents the telephone. **1876** Nikolaus Otto builds a gas-powered internal combustion engine.	**1886** German engineer Gottlieb Daimler makes a four-wheeled gasoline-fueled car. **1887** German-born U.S. engineer Emile Berliner devises the disk gramophone record.	**1893** German inventor Rudolf Diesel builds a compression-ignition, or diesel, engine. **1898** Irish–American schoolmaster John Holland builds the first modern submarine.	**1901** Italian physicist and radio pioneer Guglielmo Marconi makes the first transatlantic radio transmission. **1903** U.S. brothers Orville and Wilbur Wright make the first piloted flight in an airplane.	**1907** Belgian-born U.S. chemist Leo Baekeland invents Bakelite plastic. **1908** The first Model T Ford from U.S. industrialist Henry Ford comes off the assembly line at Detroit.
1877 German bacteriologist Robert Koch develops a method of staining bacteria in order to study them with a microscope.	**1885** French chemist Louis Pasteur produces a vaccine against rabies.	**1893** The African–American surgeon Daniel Williams performs the first open-heart surgical operation.	**1903** German surgeon Georg Perthes first uses X-rays to treat cancerous tumors.	**1906** English biologist William Bateson coins the term "genetics." **1909** Wilhelm Johannsen coins the term "gene" for the factor that carries inheritable characteristics.
1873 Scottish physicist James Clerk Maxwell publishes his theory that light is a form of electromagnetic radiation, as are radio waves and X-rays.	**1881** German scientist Hermann von Helmholtz shows that hydrogen atoms have electrical charges in whole-number portions, implying that there must be a unit of electrical charge.	**1891** Irish physicist George Stoney coins the term "electron" for the fundamental unit of electricity. **1897** English physicist J.J. Thomson identifies the electron, the first subatomic particle.	**1904** English physicist J.J. Thomson suggests the atom is a spherical mass of positively charged matter with electrons embedded in it.	**1905** German-born U.S. physicist Albert Einstein publishes his special theory of relativity.

Transparency

Timeline of Science Discoveries

Analyze important scientific discoveries from 1625 to 1825.

1. Why was the Industrial Revolution an important force in encouraging scientific research during this period? What effect did the spread of education to all classes in Europe and North America have on the process of scientific and technological research?
2. Why are some of the people in this timeline called "inventors" rather than "scientists?" Did the inventions or discoveries listed make people's lives better, or did any of them make people's lives worse? Support your conclusions.

Quiz

1 What invention of 1856 made it possible to produce steel cheaply?

2 What was the nickname of the home of the Great Exhibition?

3 Which plants did Gregor Mendel use to investigate inheritance?

4 Between which two cities did Samuel Morse send a telegraph signal in 1844?

5 Which U.S. inventor claimed that Alexander Graham Bell stole his idea for the telephone?

6 Why did Dmitri Mendeleev first try to sort chemical elements in order?

7 What is the atomic number of an element?

8 Which two biologists independently came up with the germ theory of disease?

9 Which U.S. engineer built the first assembly line?

10 What was the name of the Wright Brothers' first successful powered airplane?

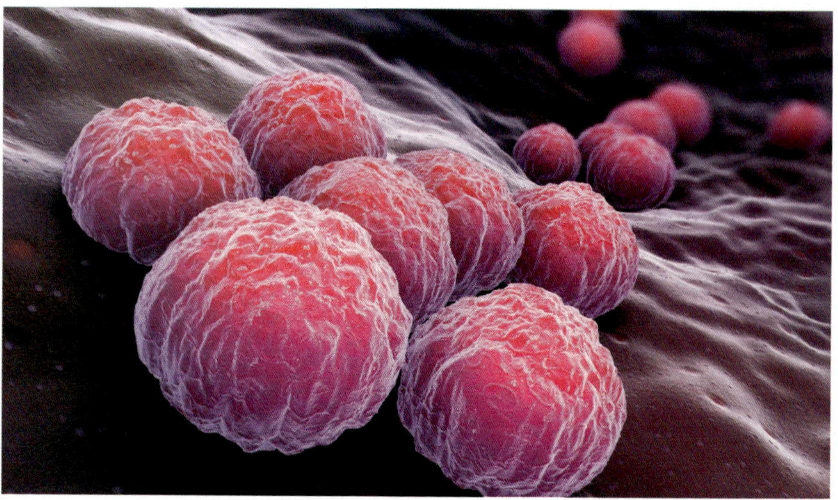

ANSWERS

1. Bessemer Converter **2.** The Crystal Palace **3.** Pea plants **4.** Washington, D.C., and Baltimore **5.** Elisha Gray **6.** He was writing a school textbook. **7.** The number of protons in an atom's nucleus **8.** Jacob Henle and Louis Pasteur **9.** Henry Ford **10.** *Flyer* or *Kitty Hawk*

Study the Sources

The history of science is a complicated subject. Historians must be able to understand scientific processes as well as the ways in which history changes because of social, economic, political, or military pressures and opportunities. Adding to the difficulty, the people who recorded advances in the past often did not understand what was actually happening in the scientific developments they were describing.

Consider a major theme discussed in this book. Topics you might choose could be steam power, transportation, or better communications.

Use the internet to find at least two descriptions and at least two images of the topic. Try to find images from European as well as North American sources. Note how people with different viewpoints portrayed different aspects as being important. Some people may be hostile to innovations, while others may be supportive, for example.

Compare the descriptions and images you find with this book. The coming of industrialization changed many aspects of life. Do you think most people's lives improved? What makes you come to that conclusion?

Key Words

alloy: a blend of a metal with another substance to give it special qualities, such as greater hardness

amplitude: the maximum extent of a vibration or wave

anode: a positively charged plate or electrode

ballast: any heavy material used to stabilize a ship, airship, or submarine

carburetor: a device in an engine that mixes air with a spray of liquid fuel

coal gas: flammable gas obtained in the distillation of coal, often as a byproduct in the preparation of coke

compressed air: air under greater pressure than the air in the environment, especially when used to power a mechanical device

conductor: any substance that allows an electric current to flow through it

diesel fuel: a fuel composed of distillates obtained in the petroleum refining process, which is ignited in engines by the heat generated from compressed air

electrolyte: a liquid or gel that contains ions that can be activated by an electrical charge

electron: a subparticle found in all atoms that carries a negative electrical charge

electronics: a branch of physics that involves the manipulation of voltages and electric currents by various devices

gasoline: a volatile, flammable liquid composed of distillates obtained in the petroleum refining process

gene: the basic unit of inheritance that controls a characteristic of an organism

genetics: the science of how characteristics are passed between generations of living things

gliders: light, unpowered aircraft designed to glide after being towed into the air or launched from a catapult

horsepower: a unit for measuring the power produced by an engine

hydrogen: a colorless, highly flammable gaseous element, the lightest of all gases and the most abundant element in the universe

Morse code: a telegraph code in which letters and numbers are represented by strings of dots and dashes

static electricity: a stationary electrical charge caused by friction that causes crackling and sparks

vaccines: preparations containing viruses or other microorganisms, introduced into the body to stimulate the formation of antibodies and build up immunity

vacuum tube: an airtight glass tube in which electricity is conducted by electrons passing through a partial vacuum from a cathode to an anode

wrought iron: a form of iron that is tough, malleable, and relatively soft. It contains usually less than 0.1 percent carbon and 1 or 2 percent of slag.

Index

LIGHTBOX

SUPPLEMENTARY RESOURCES

Click on the plus icon found in the bottom left corner of each spread to open additional teacher resources.

- Download and print the book's quizzes and activities
- Access curriculum correlations
- Explore additional web applications that enhance the Lightbox experience

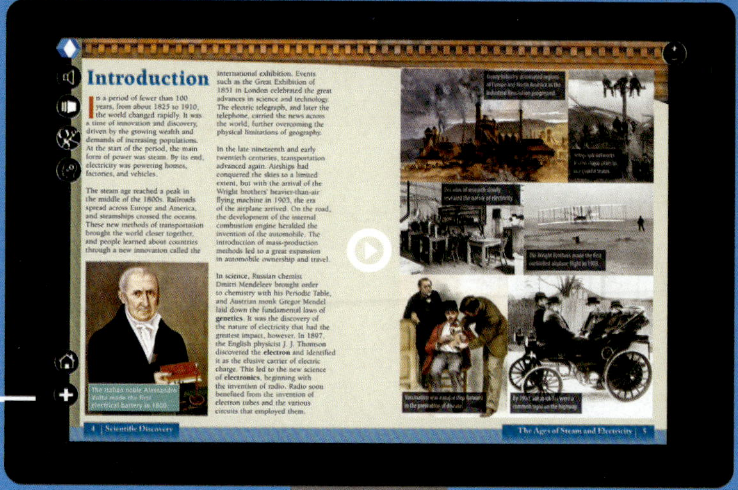

LIGHTBOX DIGITAL TITLES
Packed full of integrated media

VIDEOS

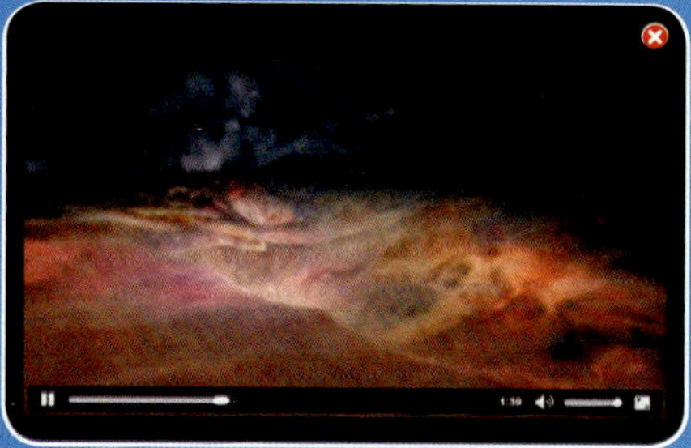

INTERACTIVE MAPS

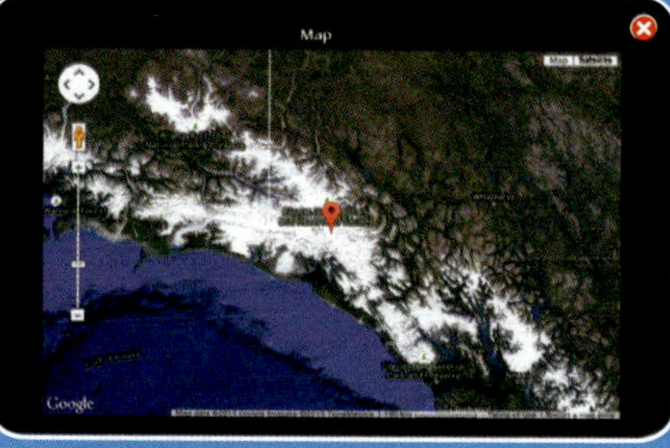

WEBLINKS

SLIDESHOWS

QUIZZES

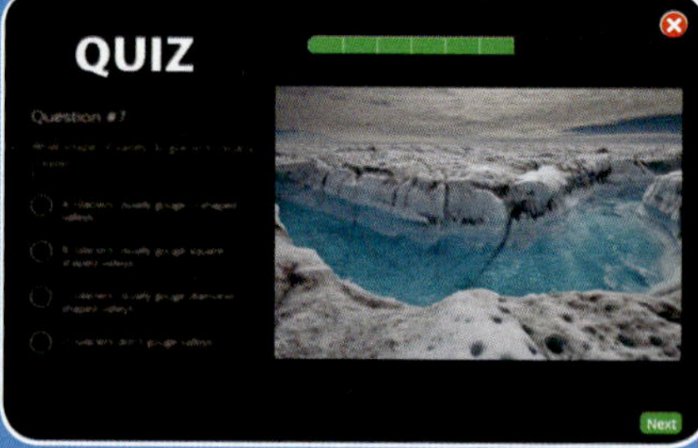

OPTIMIZED FOR
- ✓ TABLETS
- ✓ WHITEBOARDS
- ✓ COMPUTERS
- ✓ AND MUCH MORE!

Published by Smartbook Media Inc.
350 5th Avenue, 59th Floor New York, NY 10118
Website: www.openlightbox.com

First published by Brown Bear Books in 2009

Library of Congress Control Number: 2018941511

ISBN 978-1-5105-4007-1 (hardcover)
ISBN 978-1-5105-4008-8 (multi-user eBook)

Printed in Brainerd, Minnesota, United States
1 2 3 4 5 6 7 8 9 0 22 21 20 19 18

072018
121217

Project Coordinator: Heather Kissock
Art Director: Ana María Vidal

Every reasonable effort has been made to trace ownership and to obtain permission to reprint copyright material. The publisher would be pleased to have any errors or omissions brought to its attention so that they may be corrected in subsequent printings.

The publisher acknowledges Getty Images, Alamy, Newscom, and Shutterstock as its primary image suppliers for this title.